Repeal the Seventeenth Amendment, Control Washington DC

The story of the conspiracy by reformers to change our Constitution for social and economic change

Dedication

To the memory of America's Founding Fathers who created a Constitutional Republic to protect individual liberties. To Senator George F Hoar who did his best to defend their work in 1900 in the face of public passion for the promises of government expansion.

Author's Note

I first became aware of the 17th Amendment in 2003 while filming a documentary video about the damage to liberty in the year 1913. In recent years efforts have been made to change income tax rules, limit government involvement, limit the national debt and fight specific regulation. I believe the 17th Amendment is the underlying cause of most of the problems we are facing. Repeal of the 17th Amendment would be the surest method to slowly resolve the tyranny created over the last century by progressives.

Table of Contents

Chapter Seven

The Direct Democracy Reformers

Chapter Eight

Chapter Nine

The Progressive

Chapter Ten

The Outcome of the 17th

Chapter Eleven

Appendix C

Foreword

Did a small number of progressive reformers with personal and professional interests change the U.S. Constitution for their own goals?

Did they intentionally misrepresent or exaggerate the need for reform?

Why did they desire social change through scientific legislation?

Why did they want to reduce State control over federal legislation?

Did they not realize the negative effects of their proposed change?

Were they actively promoting a direct democracy or even socialism over the original republic?

Why were they modeling the German legislative reforms in America?

Why couldn't they achieve their social change experiment without the Constitutional amendment?

Did they have contempt for the Constitution and the Founders?

The details in this book will reveal the malicious, intentional and damaging Constitutional change presented by the Seventeenth Amendment.

This is the story of the attack against a great Constitution established for the natural rights of all mankind against tyranny.

Founders Alexander Hamilton, John Jay and John Madison wrote the *Federalist Papers* as a record of their opinions and debates on the topic of the Constitution. These writings were intended as an explanation of the Constitution to the States who would unanimously vote to approve it. These *Federalist Papers* are useful now as an original and primary source confirming the protection of natural rights in our Constitution against tyranny. The construction of the Senate in opposition to the U.S. House was an essential part of the design.

The research in this book is largely based on the writings preceding 1913. The statements and actions by progressive reformers reveal a coordinated attack on the Senate, the critical piece of our Constitutional Republic as constructed by the Founders. The multi-pronged military style attack against the Senate based on misrepresentation and insults can be observed through the statements of the press and the partisan politicians.

Note: Unless noted otherwise, "Amendment" refers to the 17th Amendment.

Some portions of the quotes and text have been boldened by the author as significant.

Chapter One

An Overview of the Constitution and the Amendment

The Original Constitution concerning the Senate;

The original Constitution read; Article 1 Section 3 Clause 1; The Senate of the United States shall be composed of two Senators from each state, **chosen by the legislature thereof,** for six years; and each Senator shall have one vote....

The Seventeenth Amendment change;

The Senate of the United States shall be composed of two Senators from each State, **elected by the people thereof,** for six years; and each Senator shall have one vote.

Popular election by the people? What is wrong with that?

The will of the **people were represented democratically by the popularly elected U.S. House of Representatives. The U.S. Senate was originally designed as a republic, as representatives of the State legislatures.** The rivalry between the State and the federal government was intended to control the abuse of either.

The U.S. Constitution was constructed by our Founders as a Constitutional Republic with mixed elements of democracy to insure the protection of rights of all citizens and the sovereignty of the States.

The Constitution was created by delegates of each State in the United States. The State legislatures ratified the Constitution after being assured of their sovereignty. Supreme Court Justice Joseph Story wrote about the Constitution in 1842. He called the **Senate a "Congress of Ambassadors of the States,"** as the original Old Continental Congress was comprised.

Limited, local government intended

Imagine our country where the States retained control over health, education, regulation, taxes and all other elements of government that affected our private lives. This was the condition of America until 1913, prior to the Seventeenth Amendment.

Laws that affected ordinary life were intended to be created by the States, not the federal government.

The Constitution and the first Ten Amendments, (also known as the Bill of Rights), were intended to limit the power of the federal government. The Founders always had the interest of ordinary citizen's natural rights in mind.

The founders believed laws should be debated and enforced by local governments, in the counties and the States, where the average American could be actively involved.

In the *Federalist Paper #17*, Hamilton insisted that the States would retain control over issues of ordinary citizens. Hamilton explained "private justice, supervision of agriculture, and other concern of local jurisdiction would never be desirable cares of the federal jurisdiction." He said the "troublesome intervention in these roles would not be dignified for the federal government."

The federal government was supposed to be limited to foreign relations and national economic issues. The States were assured that the federal government could not exceed its authority because the States would have their own representatives in the U.S. Senate.

The Senate was controlled by the majority of State legislatures on any issue. They could stop any excessive federal legislation that the majority of States opposed.

James Madison wrote about the importance of the States administering laws for the citizens, not the federal government. He said in *Federalist #14* "It is to be remembered that the general government is not to be charged with the whole power of making and administering laws. **Its jurisdiction is limited to certain enumerated objects. The subordinate governments (States) can extend their care to all those other subjects** which can be separately provided for will retain their due authority and activity."

The debate at the Constitutional Convention

Founding Father, John Dickinson, a Constitutional Convention delegate, and "Penman of the Revolution" described the national system of American government like the solar system. He said, "The States are like planets that are left alone to freely move in their proper orbits."[1]   James Wilson, from Pennsylvania, was the only Constitutional Convention delegate who proposed popular election of Senators. He said he was worried about the planets "devouring the national government". No other delegate endorsed his proposal for popular election of Senators.

[1] U.S. Congress Serial Set issue 5242, Debates on Constitutional Convention 1787

Alexander Hamilton was concerned the States could have excessive power but agreed that the State legislatures should appoint members of the national senate. He explained it would insure that "senators be composed of those with peculiar care and judgment and the promise of greater knowledge and extensive information to the national council"[2].

Colonel George Mason, of Virginia, the "Forgotten Founder," believed **the State legislatures ought to have means of defending against encroachments by the national government.** He said "Shall we leave the States alone un-provided with the means for this purpose?"[3]

Elbridge Gerry, a Constitutional Convention delegate from Massachusetts was one of three who refused to sign the Constitution because a *Bill of Rights* for the individual and state liberties was not originally included. He eventually drafted the *Bill of Rights*. He believed the State legislatures were most likely to provide some check in favor of commercial interest against landed interest without which oppression

[2] Hamilton, Alexander, *Federalist Paper* #27, Federalist, A Collection of Essays Written in Favor of the New Constitution, Sept 17 1787, Vol 1 and II, J A McLean

[3] Colonel George Mason U.S. Congress Serial Set issue 5242, June 7 1787 also in "Selected Articles on the Direct Election of U.S. Senators" edited by C. E. Fanning, Minneapolis, MN, H.W. Wilson, 1912 , p 71

will take place. [4]He added "no free government can last long where that is the case."

Constitutional Republic, not a Democracy

John Witherspoon, a signer of the *Declaration of Independence* wrote, **"pure democracy is subject to madness of popular rage."**

Founder James Madison and other Founders knew classic history and the friction between those who have property of many kinds and those without.

Justice Story wrote, "A **Senate, duly constituted would not only operate as a check upon the Representatives, but occasionally upon the people themselves, against their own temporary delusions and errors**. Sparta, Rome and Carthage had a Senate, long lived republics."[5]

Controlling majority passions through republic

James Madison wrote that a Constitutional Republic **protects individuals from the will of the majority of a direct democracy**. Minorities were defined literally. Minority factions could be business owners, professionals, or the poor and oppressed.

---

[4] Elbridge Gerry, Constitutional Convention U.S. Congress Serial Set issue 5242, May 31st 1787, "Debates on the Election of Senators in the Federal Convention, also "Selected Articles on Direct Election of Senators" 1912, p 94

[5] Supreme Court Justice Joseph A Story, "A Familiar Exposition of the Constitution of the U.S." Boston, T H. Webb and Co., 1842 p 66

James Madison wrote in *Federalist Paper #10.* "Republics can control passions and factions by delegation of government into divisions."

The Founders knew that popular passions of majorities had led to the downfall of other democracies and republics.

James Madison

A mob democracy government could rule against the minority and claim private rights and property for the benefit of the majority.

Sometimes majorities were created by alliances of factions with the same goals. James Madison wrote in *Federalist #10* about the danger of "factions", "**citizens in either the majority or minority could be induced with passion or interest to impose their will against the other citizens, property or community.** If the faction is a majority then the public good and private rights would be compromised."

An alliance of factions occurred about a century ago when progressives with a goal to democratize America were elected into office by popular passion.

State Delegates Controlled Federal Government Expansion Through the Senate

In the Founders' wisdom, the State legislature-controlled Senate would prevent over reach of the federal government. The State legislatures appointed or elected their own U.S. Senators to defend their interests.

Alexander Hamilton

A century after the American Revolution, the people and the State legislators had lost their memory and concern for the Constitutional protection against tyranny.

By 1913, the progressive reformers were frustrated that they could not create national social change legislation. They realized they had to remove the obstacle of the state legislature control over federal expansion.

In *Federalist* #15 Alexander Hamilton explained the benefit of rival powers, "power controlled or abridged is almost always the rival and enemy of that power by which it is controlled or abridged."

The founders never anticipated the State legislators would voluntarily and actively vote themselves out of power. They never expected the people to desire the federal government to intervene in their private lives.

A democracy was not desired

The founders understood democracies can remove rights of minority individuals. **The mobs can coerce rules on others and demand people buy, sell, or give their life, liberty or possessions.** Majority tyranny can be as restrictive as any monarchy.

In *Federalist Paper* #1 Alexander Hamilton writes **"dangerous ambition can lurk behind the mask of zeal for the rights of people**." He understood reformers would start with concerns for the masses but later become tyrants.

Mob democracy could overwhelm property rights. Alexander Hamilton describes **"real liberty as neither despotism nor extreme democracy**." He understood the common passions of majority factions could inflict their will on the minority.

James Madison in *Federalist #10* wrote, "a pure democracy is no cure for mischief of faction— nothing to check the action against the weaker party. **Democracies are incompatible with personal security and rights of property.** Democracies through history are short and violent."

The original Senate was to control popular passions of the majority

The U.S. Senate was constructed as a critical element of our Republic. The Founders expected the popularly elected U.S. House of Representatives to propose popular agendas. It was the responsibility of the Senate to evaluate the impact on the minority factions and control the momentum of popular whims. **They could not be popularly elected and effectively perform this function**.

The Senate was intended to represent the State legislatures who frequently gave instructions to their Senators during frequent correspondence. Their mission of controlling the federal government was protected by indirect voting as representatives of the States.

James Madison warned in *Federalist* #14, "the federal government is not to have the power of making and administering laws."

The Founders were in agreement that the States, as a rival power, would have primary oversight of the matters that affected the people.   They never expected the rival power of the States to be voluntarily removed.

How strongly did the Founders consider selection of the U.S. Senate by the State legislatures?

In *Federalist Paper #16* Hamilton wrote, "If the laws of the federal government did not require the intervention of the State legislatures to pass there would be open and violent exertion of unconstitutional power." Hamilton apparently expected more oversight and interest by the public in the matters of government and tyranny.

The reasons for the State selected Senators were so obvious, Alexander Hamilton wrote "It is equally unnecessary to dilate on the appointment of senators by the state legislatures. Among the various modes which might have been decided... this is recommended by the double advantage of favoring a **select appointment and at giving to the State governments as must secure the authority of the former** and may form a congenial link between the two systems."[6]

Justice Joseph Story explained the importance of State rival power in 1842, "The Senators are to be chosen by the legislature of each State. This mode has a natural tendency to **increase the just operation of the check.** The people of the States directly choose the Representatives, the Legislature, whose votes are compounded and whose mode of election is different in different states, directly chooses the Senators, so that it is impossible, that exactly the same influences, interests and feelings

[6] Alexander Hamilton *Federalist Papers* #62

should prevail in the same proportions in each branch."[7]

Alexander Hamilton encouraged the State control over the federal government. He wrote in *Federalist #9* "the proposed Constitution, so far from implying an abolition of the State governments makes them constituent parts of the national sovereignty by **allowing them a direct representation in the Senate and leaves in their possession certain exclusive and very important portions of sovereign power**."

The impact on the Constitution

The direct election of senators created an imbalance in the Constitution. **America lost the Constitutional Republic as carefully crafted by the Founders. It became the popular democracy the progressives wanted.**

The States no longer have any power to restrain the federal government which caters to the whims of the mob electorate for political gains.

The Seventeenth Amendment damaged the U.S. Constitution that limited the powers of the federal government. It also affected the Bill of Rights that insured States rights. The States lost their control over excesses of the Federal Government.

[7] Supreme Court Justice Joseph Story, A Familiar Exposition of the Constitution. p69

The impact on the country

The Seventeenth Amendment changed the country entirely. Limited government was always balanced between the separate and rival powers of the legislative government. One represented the States interests as a republic and one represented the people, as a democracy.

The damaging results of the Amendment are evident. Federal spending increased and outpaced State and local spending within a few years of passage. (See Appendix B)

The reformers sought an increased federal government and social programs. They wanted the increased government presence.

The 16th and 17th Amendments became the twin handicaps to our individual liberty. The federal taxing and federal expansion began after 1913. The federal government had the unrestrained power over States to make laws and to force the States to enforce the laws.

Individual freedom deteriorated as the States lost sovereignty over education, health and taxes. The States and the people became submissive to federal control over their property and prosperity. The primary legislation moved away from the local access and control of the people.

From the country's founding until prior to the Amendment, the federal spending was consistently 2-3% of GDP. The federal cost portion of GDP was half of State and local governments. By 1940, the federal government had matched and exceeded spending by the State and local governments.

In addition to the increased economic presence, the federal government advanced a social engineering program that has changed the character of American society

Was the Amendment necessary because the original Senate withheld important legislation?

No, the Senate actively passed significant legislation before 1913. The U.S. Senate passed the federal anti-monopoly *Sherman Anti-Trust Act* in 1890, the *Civil Service Reform* in 1883, the *Interstate Commerce Commission* in 1887, and passed laws to create *the Food and Drug Administration, Forestry Service Department of Commerce, Department of Labor*, and regulate railroads.

These major advances were insufficient for the reformers who passionately demanded more federal control.

How did the reformers promote the Seventeenth Amendment?

The reformers attacked the reputation of the Senate and State legislatures. They claimed rampant corruption of both institutions. Their propaganda involved vicious attacks on targeted Senators. The alleged scandals were minor, especially compared to present day political stories but they were sensationalized to inspire public outrage. In all ten cases, the matters were investigated by a Senate committee and the perpetrators resigned, found not guilty or expelled.

The reformers claimed their Amendment would repair corruption and bribery and special interest in politics. We know that it had an opposite effect.

A political writer, although he supported the Amendment, admitted, "Doubtless many cases against the Senate are in spirit of rank demagogy and **reckless disregard of proof, yet these accusations have found the minds of people so filled with grave apprehensions in regard to the Senate** they were readily believed."[8]

Who were the reformers and why did they want the Seventeenth Amendment?

Whether there was a genuine interest by the people or a coordinated agenda contrived by a small group was in question. "It is the testimony too of many Senators that a large number of direct vote of people resolutions which flood Congress, **bear evidence of coming from a common source,** and it being a part

---

[8] Haynes, George H., Election of Senators, New York, Henry Holt, 1906, p 164

of a **propaganda actively promoted by a few enthusiasts."**[9]

Just as our Founders predicted, factions with similar goals combined personal interests to force control of the government for their own ends. In all cases, they wanted the federal government to spend and legislate more in their interests.

Each of the factions had been denied legislation they desired because of the deliberate action of the U.S. Senate. The reformers realized they could not get government to work in their interests unless they removed the original construction of the U.S. Senate that blocked legislation as it was intended.

The specific proposals for this Constitutional Amendment came from a collection of socialists, agrarian agitators, academic social scientists, progressive newspaper editors, and politicians. Each of the factions wanted federal government intervention in their own interests.

Reformers within the factions had their own motivation; partisan gain by delivering government special projects to constituents, editorial power to influence masses, economic advantages, recognition by other progressives, and social control through scientific legislation. Their mutual interest was in destroying the original construction of the Senate.

[9] Haynes, George H Election of Senators, 1906 Henry Holt, New York, 1906 p   256

Some reformers owned, edited or manipulated the new widespread progressive national magazines and newspapers to promote their idea for reforming the U.S. Senate.

What other progressive reforms were desired?

Income taxes, prohibition, social change and federal expansion were all dreams of the progressives in the decade leading to the Seventeenth Amendment. None of these issues had a chance of passing until the State legislature control on the Senate was significantly weakened. After a decade of attacks by the popular media the reformers had already effectively diminished resistance from the State legislatures.

The progressive reformers welcomed government control of society through scientific legislation, social legislation and the equalization and distribution of wealth.

Were other progressive reformer Amendments tied to the 17th Amendment?

The Senate and the U.S. Supreme Court had previously rejected the federal income tax. Federal income tax was unconstitutional until the Constitutional Amendment in 1913. A year earlier, in1912, the income tax was promoted on a strong public outcry to "tax the rich". Up to this time the federal government expenses were supported by only the tariffs and excise taxes. The tariffs were opposed by the farmers and the excise tax was opposed by the prohibitionists. The prohibitionists needed to replace the lost tax income from alcohol.

The weekly magazine *The Commoner* owned by William Jennings Bryan, published an editorial, *Organize Now,* **"Election of Senators by popular vote is more important than empowering congress to levy an income tax."** [10]

The editorial also revealed the forced and intentional tactics, "...Majority of the democratic and republican parties favor the income tax. If proof on this point were necessary it is found in the fact that a **republican congress has been forced by public sentiment to submit an income tax amendment**."[11]

Bryan said, "We really need an income tax only as an alternative to tariff exaction and there is no escape from tariff exactions until the senate is made answerable to the public."[12]

[10] Bryan, William Jennings, Evening Post, *The Commoner, "Organize Now"* page 6 Vol. 9 No. 31 Aug 13 1909

[11] Bryan, William Jennings, Evening Post, *The Commoner,* "Organize Now" page 6 Vol. 9 No. 31 Aug 13 1909

[12] Bryan, William Jennings, Evening Post, *The Commoner,* page 6 Vol. 9 No. 31 Aug 13 1909

The reformers were successful in 1913. Also in 1913 the Federal Reserve Act, the Federal Trade Commission Act and the Revenue Act were passed.

In 1919 the reformers finally achieved prohibition of alcohol (18th Amendment). It was repealed in 1933, (21st Amendment).

The Women's Suffrage, {women's right to vote, 19th Amendment} was not uniquely a progressive effort. It was supported by conservatives also.[13]

The progressives were voted out of office after 1919. Their legacy of income taxation and federal government growth at the expense of State sovereignty remains. A list of historical federal income tax brackets and the continuous revisions is in Appendix F.

Didn't the reformers realize the U.S. was a Constitutional republic?

Every promoter of the reforms dismissed the representative **republic** side of our country's founding and focused the public mind on the democracy side of our founding. It was the careful balance between the two that controlled federal

---

[13] The Constitution did not prevent women from voting. Certain States began to legislate against the right of women to vote after the Constitution was ratified. New Jersey was the last to succumb to factions to prevent the women's right to vote.

tyranny. They used the popular appeal of democracy to further their own cause.

An 1894 article forecast the warning against tampering with the Constitution and the Founders, "A century of experience has demonstrated the wisdom of their marvelous plan. But a new school of politicians has now appeared who profess to believe that the fathers were mistaken in their theory of the surest foundation of our national republic."[14]

Founder, James Madison wrote a "**Constitutional Republic, not a direct democracy would protect the individual from the will of the majority.**"

How was it achieved so quickly?

The reformers misrepresented the indirectly elected Senate as a mistake that needed to be corrected. The propaganda of direct democracy was appealing to the masses that had lost their fear of government tyranny after decades of liberty. The American population was a century removed from the Revolution and tyrannical government abuse.

It was the decades-long propaganda attacks against the State legislatures and the Senate that allowed the reformers to succeed.

[14] Edmunds, George F, "Should Senators be Elected by the People?" Forum, 18;270-8 Nov 1894, www.unz.org

A 1909 author described the widespread appeal, "during the past decade the agitation in favor of this amendment has acquired such force and definiteness that to many its adoption seems close at hand."[15]

There was limited defensive debate before or during the ratification process. The proponents of the Amendment rushed its passage while passion was inflamed. "For several decades the wisdom of such an amendment has been under discussion in the press and in legislatures. For some years the demand for it has been great, general and irresistible. The Senate found that it could not stand in the way of reform much longer. If it had not yielded and acted favorably, the legislatures, by their resolutions would within another year or two force a submission of the amendment."[16]

Couldn't States directly elect their Senators before the Seventeenth Amendment?

Yes, in fact 29 States already elected Senators by the people. The leading proponent of the Amendment declared without explanation that "optional voting was not an acceptable option." The reformers insisted on a Constitutional Amendment.

---

[15] Haynes, George H, Election of Senators, p 132

[16] Bryan, William Jennings, *Chautauqua*, 67; 105-7 July 1912

A political scientist and Amendment supporter failed to adequately explain their insistence, "but the teaching of both theory and experience is that without amendment of Constitution genuine popular control over Senatorial elections cannot be realized." [17]

The Seventeenth Amendment simply made it permanent and forced it on States that opposed it. It was an experiment that the reformers wanted permanent. If it had not become an Amendment to the Constitution, the States could later correct the experiment with State legislation. When the federal government inevitably exceeded Constitutional authority there were few remedies for the States to correct the error.

The fact that States had already made laws to allow the citizens to vote for Senators reveals that the progressive reformers were not interested in individual rights, but instead promoting federal power.

Was the direct election of senators a socialist goal?

It seemed to be accelerated by the socialists. The actual **elimination of the U.S. Senate** was proposed in 1911 by the first socialist U.S. Representative, Victor Berger of Milwaukee Wisconsin. Milwaukee

---

[17] Haynes, George H. The Election of Senators, p 262

was already operating under a socialist administration in 1911.

Only seven weeks after Rep. Berger's outrageous proposal the Senate approved the proposal for direct election of Senators.

Did the founders predict this?

No, they never expected the State legislatures to voluntarily ratify a Constitutional Amendment to surrender their power to the federal government.

Alexander Hamilton's inability to forecast federal encroachment is documented in *Federalist Paper* #17. He said it "will always be far easier for the State governments to encroach on the federal than for the federal government to encroach on the States."

Hamilton believed the people would protect the States from any encroachment of the federal government. The Founders predicted a populace that remained vigilant in protecting their country and their rights. They had the personal experience of living under tyranny. They did not predict the people taking freedom for granted and giving power to the government. They did not anticipate the progressive movement and desire to legislate social change.

Why did some reformers desire social change?

The reformers were the product of a changing world in the 19th and early 20th centuries. Evolution studies, social gospel and social sciences led to a momentum of an evolving culture. These changes extended to social, economic and cultural evolution. Constitutional changes and scientific legislation were popular in Europe.

Karl Marx and Fredrich Engels wrote of the alleged natural evolution of capitalism toward communism as a social and economic ideal. Many academicians were captivated by their economic theories. Marx wrote a column for a New York newspaper to promote the ideas he expected would begin in America.

The new academic sciences of economics, psychology, sociology and political science promoted the concept of scientific legislation in the universities.

The "Wisconsin Idea" was promoted as a model of a statewide social experiment. The University of Wisconsin led the nation in scientific legislation.

The progressive reformers believed society could be and should be changed. Many popular writers, editors and politicians believed and promoted the cause also.

The Founders had predicted the intervention of man's desire to control others through the government. In *Federalist Paper #51* James Madison wrote **"If men were angels no government would be necessary, if angels governed, no external or internal control would be necessary.** The great difficulty is to enable the government to control the governed and oblige it to control itself."

Why didn't the church leadership speak out against social control advocates?

The churches in America were well attended and could influence public opinion. The progressives had already inserted social gospel goals in major denominations and seminaries. The ecumenical organizations promoted the social gospel as a new interpretation of biblical teaching. Under the new progressive leadership the major protestant denominations moved in unison toward embracing global social goals.

Was there partisan political motivation for the Amendment?

The Democrat Party and People's Party platform promoted direct election of senators in 1900, 1904, and 1908. It first appeared in the People's Party Platform in 1892 and 1896.[18]

A newspaper article reflected the partisan promotion in 1911. It stated, "The house democrats at Washington have definite plans to benefit the

---

[18] Haynes, George H., Election of Senators, p 106

country. They have planned their work and will work their plans sending to the senate important bills that must be endorsed or the senate will have to bear the blame of failure to endorse. The democrats, sure they are right, are pushing vigorously. Senate republicans may delay but delays are dangerous to their party. The people everywhere are watching and thousands in every state will remember at the polls in November of next year the records made at Washington in 1911. In Chariton County, democrats generally are feeling pretty good over the outlook."[19]

The democrats had little to lose from embracing the new progressive reforms agenda. They had lost the Senate in 23 of 26 previous Congressional sessions prior to the amendment. William Jennings Bryan, a progressive Democrat was the candidate for both the Progressive Party and the Democrat Party in 1896. He is said to have led the Democrat party away from limited government and toward progressive reforms.

Bryan declared, "In 1900, 1904 and 1908 the democrat party favored the election of US. Senators by a direct vote of the people. **And we regard this reform as the gateway to other national reforms**. In this year of 1912 the Democratic Party stands consistently for real progressive measures. ... The first formal suggestion made in congress for the

[19] "Democrats Doing Right", April 21 1911, p 1 Chariton Courier

election of the U.S. Senators by popular vote was made by a democrat. The first joint resolution ever reported for the submission of an amendment for direct election of senators was submitted by a democrat congress. Income tax and election of Senators by the people."[20]

William Jennings Bryan complained "The subject {direct election of Senators} was ignored by the Republican National Convention in 1900, ignored in 1904 proposition and repudiated in 1908. The Republican National Convention rejected the plank 866 to 114."[21]

The Republicans had controlled the U.S. Senate by a wide majority for decades. They won 23 of 26 Congressional sessions in the prior 52 years. In 1907 the Democrats blamed the economic recession on the Republicans failure to allow free silver to inflate the currency. The Democrats gained seats in 1910.

By 1911 the progressives had the votes necessary to propose the income tax and direct election of senators amendments. Speeches in Congress for and against the Amendment by party, are listed in Appendix E.

[20] Bryan, William Jennings, *The Commoner*, Editorial, October 18 1912 p 6

[21] Bryan, William Jennings Speeches of William Jennings Bryan, p 112

Were there republican progressive reformers?

Yes, Robert M. Lafollette Sr., a Republican U.S. Senator from Wisconsin was an active promoter for progressive causes and created the *National Republican Progressive League.* By 1908, many politicians in both parties described themselves as progressive. It was a popular political movement. In 1912 all of the Presidential Candidates described themselves as progressive. Two of the three were Republicans. The progressive influence in the Republican party dissipated within a decade.

Why did the State legislatures approve and ratify their own loss of control over the Senate?

By the time the 17th Amendment was sent to the States for ratification, the popular passion was exuberant based on the sensational journalism. The Amendment passed with shockingly little debate or controversy.

The States approved the amendment because of the overwhelming passion stirred up by the reformers. Many of the elected State representatives were themselves progressive reformers. It was truly the "popular madness" that the founders described.

Didn't anyone stand up for the original Constitution construction and the ideas of the Founding Fathers?

Most Americans seemed to be sold on the promise of more democracy. They hadn't maintained their fear of tyranny. Alexander Hamilton recognized the importance of the citizens understanding the Constitution to defend the country. He wrote in *Federalist Paper* #16 "the people and the judges to rise in **defense of the Constitution as long as the people were enlightened enough to distinguish illegal usurpation of authority** and the judges were not in conspiracy."

Republican Senators Henry Cabot Lodge, Elihu Root, and George F Hoar were the most outspoken against the Amendment and understood the damage.

Why were there so many Constitutional Amendments in that time period?

Some reformers were promoting a direct democracy through the *initiative and referendum* process by the citizens in each State. The direct democracy movement was led by a group in the western States following an idea of a Swiss socialist. They would inspire Constitutional revisions in many State Constitutions also. More details about direct democracy advocates are provided in a later chapter.

When was the Seventeenth Amendment ratified?

It was officially ratified April 8 1913, although some question the legitimacy. The initial announcement of ratification was made in May 1913 by one of the chief supporters, Secretary of State, and Democrat progressive reformer, William Jennings Bryan.

As late as 2012-2014 a few States joined the ratification completed a century earlier. In recent years, other States have proposed to repeal it.

The Historical Timeline of the 17th Amendment is listed in Appendix A.

How did the relationship between the State legislatures and the Senate change?

Prior to the 17th Amendment, the Senators discussed federal issues with the State legislatures on a regular basis. They answered to the State legislature and depended on their votes for re-election. If the Senators were not in agreement with the State legislatures, sometimes they resigned or changed their position.

After the Seventeenth Amendment, the relationship was no longer essential. The Senators did not have to win the votes of the State legislatures to retain their seat. The State legislatures had no power to insist that Senators represent their State's interests. Current State legislators have commented that they rarely communicate with the U.S. Senators.

The following is the story of how the Seventeenth Amendment was created and ratified. It reveals the corruption and manipulation of popular opinion and the intentional neglect of the reasons behind the original Senate construction.

Chapter Two

A Question of State Sovereignty

The *Declaration of Independence* was the first document unanimously agreed upon by the thirteen "United States of America." It was adopted by Congress on July 4, 1776. State sovereignty and protection of each State and the citizen's natural rights was the primary goal.

It reads, "We therefore, the representatives of the United States of America, in General Congress, assembled, appealing to the Supreme Judge of the world for the rectitude of our intentions, do, in the name, and by the authority of the good people of these colonies, solemnly publish and declare that these united colonies are, and of right ought to be **free and independent states**; that they are absolved for all allegiance to the British Crown and that all political connection between them and the state of Great Britain, is and ought to be totally dissolved; and that as **free and independent states**, they have full power to levy war, conclude peace, contract alliances, establish commerce and to do all other acts and things which **independent states** may of right do. And for the support of this declaration, with a firm reliance on the protection of Divine Providence, we mutually pledge to each other our lives, our fortunes and our sacred honor."[22]

Establishing State Sovereignty

Based on the *Federalist Papers* and other records we know the founders studied the histories and failures of other democracies and republics in Athens, Rome, Sparta, and Great Britain. They believed they had created a Constitution to withstand the errors of those valid attempts. They believed in the natural rights given to man by the creator, of life, liberty and pursuit of happiness, the *Theory of Natural Law*. These ideas were promoted by John Locke who influenced many of our founders. The *Declaration of Independence* was a statement of their belief in the natural law and their intent to honor it. "'we hold these truths to be self-evident, that all men are created equal and endowed by the creator with certain unalienable rights, that among these are life, liberty and the pursuit of happiness."[23]

[22] Declaration of Independence, Conclusion

[23] Declaration of Independence, Introduction

The *Declaration of Independence* was based on the legal liberty provided British subjects by the *Magna Carta* of 1215 and the *Declaration of Rights* in 1689.

After the American Revolution was won in 1781 the independent States retained an intentionally weak federal government through the *Articles of Confederacy of States.* The States remained sovereign. George Washington retired and returned to Mount Vernon. He refused to become the king of America. The States operated under the *Articles of Confederation.*

Years later, Founders James Madison and Alexander Hamilton encouraged the Continental Congress to make improvements on the *Articles of Confederacy* and assure further guarantee of States rights. The Constitution was ratified unanimously by the States with the *Bill of Rights*. The *Bill of Rights,* the first ten amendments, restrain the power of the federal government.

Alexander Hamilton wrote in *Federalist Paper* #16 "If the execution of the laws of the national government should not require the intervention of the State legislatures if they were to pass into immediate operation upon the citizens themselves, the government could not interrupt their progress without open and violent exertion of constitutional power."

The Founders understood the potential for abuse of power. They assumed that abuse would come from the States, not the federal government. They also realized the representation of the State governments was critical. In *Federalist Paper* #54 James Madison wrote "possibility of injury from the State legislatures it is an evil, but is an evil which could not be avoided without excluding the States from a place in the national government... it would have deprived State governments of that absolute safeguard which they will enjoy under this provision."

Alexander Hamilton stated in *Federalist Paper* #22 "when the concurrence of a large number is required for a national act we are safe, nothing improper is likely to be done. The foundations of a national government depend on delegated authority with consent of the people."

In 1788, the Constitution was ratified by all the States. George Washington was unanimously elected President. The United States was designed as a representative republic of sovereign States, not a pure democracy.

Defending State Sovereignty

One of the primary spokesmen against the Amendment since 1890 was Senator George F Hoar. He explained, "The State legislatures are the bodies of men most interested of all others to preserve State jurisdiction—it is well that the members of one branch of the legislature should look to them for their reelection and it is a great security for the rights of the States. Here in the State legislature is found the great security against the encroachment upon the rights of the states."[24]

Senator George F Hoar described the powers of sovereignty divided between the nation and the States. "For all purposes of commerce and foreign intercourse, we are a Republic. For all domestic government 44 republics are free to seek its own welfare, make laws, regulate institutions in republican liberty."[25]

Senator Hoar understood the impact of the Amendment. His logical reasoning did not match the emotional appeal of democracy on the national media. Popular democratic election was an easier message to sell.

Hoar added, "The State legislatures are the depositories of the sovereignty of the States. Do you propose to strip the State legislatures of any other function of their sovereignty?" [26]

Senator Elihu Root addressed the New York State legislature in 1909. He understood the war against State sovereignty as part of the progressive agenda. He told them, "I am opposed to everything that tends

[24] Senator Hoar, George F, April 3 1893, Congressional Record 25 101-110, April 6,7 1893

[25] Sen. George F Hoar, Sen. Doc 25 1890, 54th Congress

[26] Hoar, George F, Congressional. Record 25 101-110 April 6,7 1893 p 54 also "Selected Articles on Direct Election of Senators" edited C. E Fanning, Minneapolis, 1912

to belittle to discredit or to weaken the authority of the legislatures of the States. You cannot take power away from privileged public bodies without having the character of those bodies deteriorate. I am opposed to the direct election of Senators as I am opposed to the initiative and referendum because they are things based upon the idea that the people cannot elect legislatures whom they trust."[27]

Senator George F Hoar warned about the proposed changes of election of Senators, "Such a method of election would essentially change the character of the Senate as conceived by the convention that framed the constitution and the people who adopted it. It would transfer practically the selection of the members of this body from the legislatures, who are entrusted with all legislative powers of the States, to bodies having no other responsibilities, whose election cannot be regulated by law, whose members act by proxy, whose tenure of office is for a single day, whose votes and proceedings are not recorded, who act under no personal responsibility."[28]

Senator Hoar also realized that the popular elections and the masses in large cities could eventually change the boundaries of representative districts, overwhelming the influence of voters in the rural

---

[27] Senator Elihu Root, address to New York legislature 1909 *Independent* 66;382 Feb. 18 1909 "Going Back to the People" also p 114 "Selected Articles" edited C E Fanning, 1912

[28] Senator Hoar, George F, Congressional Record 25: 101-110 April 3, 6,7 1893

areas. He said, "It will transfer the seat of political power in the great States now distributed evenly over their territory to the great cities and masses of population." He was correct. After decades of increasing popular control, the majorities in the urban areas have overwhelmed the rural areas. The number of Congressional seats in the popularly elected U.S. House had already doubled by 1910. The States were permitted to redistrict the Congressional seats in any way they wished.

It would be easy to influence a city of moderately interested voters through a newspaper editorial column. It was more difficult to influence State legislators who were more personally aware of the history and issues. Hoar said, "It will create new temptations to fraud, corruption and other illegal practices and in close cases will give rise to numerous election contests which must tend seriously to weaken the confidence of the people in the Senate."

Hoar also realized the transfer of power in elections. "It will place these elections under complete national control. It will result in the overthrow of the whole scheme of the Senate and the whole scheme of the national Constitution as designed and established by the framers of the Constitution."[29]

---

[29] Senator Hoar, George F, U.S. Congressional Record, 25 101-110 April 3, 6,7 1893, also p 42 "Selected Articles" edited by C E Fanning 1912

Senator Porter J McCumber was personally persuaded by the popular appeal of democratically elected senators but cautioned, ".. no man can deny that the new system opens up a wonderful field of opportunity for both the millionaire and the demagogue—a field broader than any one known in our political history."[30]

Other Senators and advocates of the Amendment were possibly foolishly unaware of the true intent. "The proposed amendment in no respect changes the relation now existing between the states respectively and the national government the existing sovereignty of each in its respective sphere is not in the slightest manner disturbed."[31] History and statistics has revealed how wrong he was.

Another advocate for the Amendment, Senator David Turpie of Indiana revealed the lack of understanding of the principles of representative government, "The time has come in the history of the country when one branch of government, the legislative department should be placed more directly under the control of the people of the several states." [32]

[30] Sen. McCumber, Porter J, Congressional Record 47; 1879 - 1884 (June 12 1911) reported in p 69 "Selected Articles", edited by C E Fanning, 1912

[31] Senator Mitchell, John H, "Election of Senators by Popular Vote, *Forum* 21; 385-97 June 1896 also "Selected Articles, 1912, p 110

[32] Sen. Turpie, David, 53rd Congress 3rd Session, Dec 3 1894 Senate Misc. Doc No 1 53rd Congress 3rd Session Dec 3 1894

The people and the leaders had not remained vigilant and knowledgeable about the Constitution and the well balanced design. They tampered without understanding.

A political scientist wrote arrogantly in 1906, "the protest that under popular elections the Senate would fail to secure representation of the States is academic and fallacious." [33] He believed that the gains of fewer rich men, less party influence, greater political education of the people better state legislatures, less party spirit, less corruption would outweigh the losses. [34] History would prove him wrong in every count.

The Attack on the Reputation of State Legislatures

The same writer in 1906 acknowledged the alleged dishonesty in Senate elections may be related to the 1866 Federal Law. "There is indisputable proof that a number of legislatures have been tainted by bribery in the interest of senatorial candidates, and that it is evil has not been lessened but rather increased since the enactment of the law of 1866. For nearly 70 years after the Constitution not once was the senate called upon to investigate a senator's

[33] Haynes, George H, Election of Senators, p 267 264

[34] Haynes, George H, Election of Senators, p 172,173, 184

election. Ten Senators between 1857-1899, 8 cases exonerated, 2 resigned."[35]

He forecast wrongly that direct election of Senators would "elevate the tone of state and municipal politics and promote home rule and give the States better legislatures."[36]

The Surprising Relinquishing of Power from the States to the Federal Government

Over twenty State legislatures had called for a direct vote for Senate elections before 1913. California and Nevada conducted referendum votes on the issue. In 1906, a conference was called by the Iowa governor in Des Moines for States to discuss a strategy for direct vote for Senate. There is little explanation for this forfeiture of responsibility of the State officials to their office and to the Constitution. (Appendix D lists the States that demanded Direct Election of Senators.)

[35] Haynes, George, H, "The Election of Senators., 1909

[36] Haynes, George H, Election of Senators p 187, 197, 199

Chapter Three

The Leading Defenders and Their Reasons Against the Amendment

Senator George F Hoar was the leading defender in the early years of the progressive attack on the Senate. George F Hoar was a Senator from Massachusetts between 1877 until his death in 1904. He had been a U.S. House Representative from 1869 to 1877. He fought political corruption, he argued for African American voting rights and he was in favor of women's voting rights. He was the grandson of Roger Sherman, who signed the *Declaration of Independence* and the *U.S. Constitution*.

Senator George F Hoar admired the Founding Fathers and their experiences. He stated, "The men of that day had many great advantages for this work. They had conducted a great revolution. To prepare for it that they had been engaged for a century in discussing the principles on which self-government is founded and by which constitutional liberty is secured."[37]

Senator George F. Hoar, 1826-1904, Republican Massachusetts,, , U.S House 1869-1877, U.S. Senate, 1877-1904,

When Senator Hoar died in 1904 the Senate lost a great defender. Unfortunately the people never feared the impact of the coming federal tyranny. Many generations had lived in individual freedom and felt secure based on the original work of the Founders.

[37] Senator Georg F Hoar, Congressional Record, 25, 101-110, April 3 1893

Another defender of the original Constitution was Senator Henry Cabot Lodge, who was known as the "Scholar of the Senate". Lodge was opposed to the direct election of Senators, free silver, and income taxation. He was one of the 21 Senators targeted in the *Cosmopolitan Magazine* 1906 muckraking series, "Treason of the Senate". That series will be explored later in this text.

Senator Henry Cabot Lodge, 1850-1924 Republican, Massachusetts, U. S. House, 1887-1893, U.S. Senator 1893-1924,

Lodge was a conservative Republican who co-wrote an elections bill with George F. Hoar in 1890 to allow African American voting rights. Their bill was reportedly stopped by Democrats in the U.S. Senate. Lodge stated the direct election of Senators "struck at the foundation of the national government". [38] He tried to explain the logic of the original construction of the Senate, having two distinct bodies, elected by different constituencies. Few other Senators defended the Senate construction or their own reputations maligned by some progressive reformers.

[38] Senator Lodge, Henry Cabot, *The Washington Times*, Feb. 6 1911

A newspaper noted the absence of opposition to the amendment during the ratification process in 1912, "There is some opposition to the ratification of the Constitutional Amendment but as yet the opposition has taken no definite organization form." ... "The friends of the Constitutional Amendment for the election of Senators by the people direct instead of by State Legislatures will keep up an organization and use its influence to get the matter promptly before the legislative bodies of the different States as soon as they meet."[39]

The following are the reasons for defending the original Senate construction.

Reason #1 State selected Senators were agreed by the Founders as the best way to check federal expansion over States rights.

Senator Hoar implored, "The State legislatures are the bodies of men most interested of all others to preserve the State jurisdiction. It is well that members of one branch should look to them for re-election and it is a great security for the rights of States."[40]

The Founders created the Constitution to prevent the majority from oppressing those not in power.

---

[39] George Clinton, "Battle Not Ended", The *Bemidji Daily Pioneer*, June 21 1912 page 3

[40] Senator George Hoar, Senate Doc 232 59th Congress 1st session referenced May 23 1908

Any minority faction can be at risk, the weak, the rich, the poor, the educated.

The Founders studied examples of government systems that survived long term. They chose a republic with a senate. The house would be democratically elected, but the Senate would be elected by a separate body indirectly so as not to be affected by popular passion.

The Congressional Record includes a well stated essay in 1890, "The great advantage of two branches of legislature is secured not only by having two houses, but by having two houses represented by different constituents and interests."[41]

Reason #2 The Founders believed the Senate should not be popularly elected like the U.S. House.

A news article about a Georgetown University debate on this issue reported, "The students decided that the Constitution should not be amended with the direct vote for Senators because "the framers of the Constitution knew what they were about when they placed the election of United States Senators in the keeping of the Legislatures of the various States. Americans have not grown any less corrupt during the past century and that if the Founders of the Government thought it safer to have Senators

[41] Edmunds, George F, "Senate Doc 25, 54th Congress Nov 13 1890

elected by the States, they were probably right, for their day and the present generation."[42]

Representative Boyd Winchester, a Democrat from Kentucky accurately stated "If the two houses were elected for the same period and by the same electors, they would amount in practice to little more than two committees of the same house."

Senator Hoar continued to describe why the members of the Senate are one of the real balances of our system. "The Senate is less democratic than the House and consequently less sensible to transient phases of public opinion; but it is not less sensible than the House of its ultimate accountability to the people, and is quite as obedient to the more permanent and imperative judgments of the public mind.[43]

Reason #3 The Senate was intended to be more thoughtful and deliberate slower without the passion of popular sentiment. The Senate had effectively filled that role until 1913.

Senator George F Hoar reminded others of the objective evaluation of the Senate by foreign statesmen. He spoke to the Senate, "Wherever there can be found an expression of admiration for the

[42] *The Washington Times*, Feb. 27 1902 page 1

[43] U.S. Rep. Boyd Winchester, *The House and the Election of Senators*, Arena 24 14-20 July 1900,

American Constitution in the works of any great writer or thinker at home or abroad it will be found at the admiration on the deliberate and indirect action of the popular will instead of its immediate rapid, inconsiderate and direct action..." [44]

Founder James Madison stated the Senate would consist in its proceeding with "more coolness, more system and more wisdom than the popular branch."[45]

An article in 1908 described the protection provided by the Senate construction, "For over a hundred years amid all the storms of party passion... the Senate has maintained its distinctive features, calm, dignified, patriotic ..**The Senate has fulfilled** ardent hopes and verified profound wisdom of its creators by its ability to check democratic recklessness of the House and executive usurpation....**protecting the country against the dangers and confusion which arise from the enactment of laws which did not reflect the calm judgment of the people but the temporary and transient folly or madness of the hour** and maintaining unimpaired the rights of the states and national government."[46]

[44] Senator George Hoar, Congressional Record 25 April 3 1893, 101-110

[45] James Madison, Constitutional Convention

[46] O'Neal, Emmet, "Election of U.S. Senators by the People." *North American Review* 188; 700-15 Nov 1908 www.unz.org

Reason #4 The direct election of Senators would not reduce corruption but probably enable special interest and dishonesty.

The State legislatures supervised elections and documented voting processes and records for Senators until 1913. For seventy years there was no report of corruption, the few cases of bribery were investigated thoroughly and the senators removed if the facts revealed corruption. It is far easier to investigate the relations between a candidate and the legislators than a candidate and a statewide population.

George F Hoar realized the opportunity for fraud and crime. He said "It is the purpose and the effect of this Constitutional amendment to overthrow state autonomy ... there will be larger opportunities for fraud and crime in elections. They will be easy to commit and hard to be inquired into." [47]

He was proven correct in the attack on State autonomy. A century after continuous erosion, States have almost no power to control the federal intrusion.

Reason #5 The State deadlocks could be effectively resolved by other tie breaking voting options.

---

[47] Sen. George F Hoar, Sen. Doc 232 59th Congress 1st session, (noted on May 23, 1908)

The deadlocks largely became an issue after the Federal Law of 1866 that prescribed the process for the state legislatures. The law could have been easily changed to allow the governors a vote to break the tie. It was not a legitimate reason to change the Constitution.

In Congressional Testimony Senator Weldon B Heyburn of Idaho answered the issue of state deadlocks, ""I will put it nearly 99 times out of 100- they perform that duty within the first two or three days after they commence to vote. I have the official figures as to that." [48] The 1% of deadlocks could have been resolved by other legislation dealing with elections.

Reason #6 The reformers had more progressive changes in mind to enact social and economic changes that were not consistent with the U.S. Constitution.

Senator Hoar warned of the anticipated negative repercussions to the country if the Amendment passed and the reformers were free to launch federal programs. He said, "I think it can be established... that the change is in itself a change in principle and essence of the most vital character and that its logic will lead to other changes equally vital and essential". ..

---

[48] Senator Weldon B Heyburn, Congressional Record, 46; 2768-75 Feb. 17 1911, "Selected Articles," C E Fanning, ed, 1912, p 66

"It will result in the overthrow of the whole scheme of the Senate and in the end of the whole scheme of the National Constitution as designed and established by the framers of the Constitution and the people who adopted it."[49]

William Jennings Bryan, the principle Amendment supporter admitted **"It would be difficult to overestimate the strategic advantages of this reform** {direct vote for Senators} for since every bill must receive the sanction of the Senate as well as the House of Representatives before it can become law, no important remedial legislation of a national character is possible until the Senate is brought into harmony with the people"[50]

Reason #7 The Amendment would change the government from a representative republic into a form where minority interests could be trampled by majority factions.

Senator Hoar courageously continued to speak in the face of the overwhelming public passion at the moment, "**I am not afraid to say to the American people that it is dangerous to trust any great power of government to their direct or inconsiderate control.** I am not afraid to tell them not only that their sober second thought is better

---

[49] Sen. Hoar, George G. Senate Doc 232 59th Congress 1st session, (noted May 23 1908)

[50] Bryan, William Jennings, Speeches of William Jennings Bryan Vol. 2 p 70

than their hasty action, but that a government which is exposed to the hasty action of a people is the worst and the best government on earth. **No matter how excellent may be the individual the direct, immediate, hasty action of any mass of individuals on earth is the pathway to ruin."**

He was proven correct when short term partisan federal control has led to national tyrannical legislation over private property, health and education.

Chapter Four

The Leading Progressive Reformers

William Jennings Bryan, politician

One of the most prolific of speakers on progressive and populist issues was William Jennings Bryan, an attorney and politician from Nebraska.

William Jennings Bryan, a progressive Democrat, had a personal motivation for the direct election of the Senate. He was elected twice to the U.S. House of Representatives from Nebraska. In 1894 he chose to run for U S. Senate instead. However, the Republicans had the majority in the Nebraska legislature and did not vote for him. After that time, he often spoke and wrote for the direct election of senators.

Bryan's important contribution to the 17th Amendment was confirmed by Senator Chauncey M

Depew, "This movement has received more impetus from the advocacy of Mr. Bryan than from any other cause during the half century since the war."[51]

Bryan's Presidential candidacy was endorsed by the People's Party and the Democrats in 1896. He was the Democrat candidate for president in 1896, 1900 and 1904.

After his election loss in 1900, Bryan started publishing *The Commoner,* a weekly newspaper in Nebraska to promote his opinions.

Bryan dramatized the popular debates with villains being the corporations or legislatures and the victims being the people. The following is an excerpt of a speech in 1894, "we know that today great corporations exist in our States and that these corporations are different than what they used to be 100 years ago are able to compass the election of their tools and their agents through the instrumentality of legislatures as they could not if senators were elected directly by the people."[52]

The speech was given at the same time as his failed attempt to become a Senator.

---

[51] Senator Chauncey M Depew, Congressional Record, 46;1335-9 January 24 1911, (archive.org)

[52] Congressional Record, 26; 7775 July 20 1894 also, "Selected Articles" C. E. Fanning editors, 1912 p 81

William Jennings Bryan

A foreword to a Bryan biography gushed with typical praise by a supporter. "He is magnetic, he is pleasant to the eye, to the ear, and soothes by this presence. His is cool and flawless in temper. His intellect is rather military than philosophical. He makes weapons with all he knows political; he refuses no call to speak."[53]

It was Bryan that is credited with changing the Democrat platform into a progressive platform. The progressive platform included free silver, abolition of national banks, graduated income tax and direct election of Senators. The variety of issues he added to the platform was the subject of political comics.

In one of the biographies written by himself and his wife, Mary Baird Bryan, they quoted an admirer of

[53] Ogilvie, J.S., foreword, <u>Life and Speeches of William Jennings Bryan</u>, New York, J.S. Ogilvie Publishing Co   p16

Bryan calling him, "the greatest liberal and progressive leader in America."[54]

Bryan admitted larger goals, "The Democratic platform very properly describes the **popular election of Senators as gateway to other national reforms."** [55]

After a decade in the public's attention he was a subject of critics and comics who did not anticipate his success. Some believe he was the subject portrayed by the cowardly lion in L. Frank Baum's The Wonderful Wizard of Oz.[56]

Walter Lippmann described Bryan as "too simple for the task of statesmanship. His voice crying in the wilderness but a voice that did not understand its own message."[57]

Illustration: Bryan depicted foolishly as Boy Orator with a diminishing act "About Run Down" in W.A Rogers cartoon October 31 1896. The cartoonist was in error. Bryan had decades of progressive reforms ahead.

[54] Bryan, William Jennings and his wife, The Memoirs of William Jennings Bryan, 1925 Chicago, John C Winston Co., p 493 quoting Wayne C Williams.

[55] Bryan, William Jennings Speeches of William Jennings Bryan, vol. 2 p 113

[56] Baum, L Frank, The Wonderful Wizard of Oz, Chicago, Geo. M Hill Co, 1900

[57] Lippmann, Walter, Preface to Politics, New York, Mitchell Kennerley, 1914 p 101

HARPER'S WEEKLY

JOURNAL OF CIVILIZATION

NEW YORK, SATURDAY, OCTOBER 31, 1896.

ABOUT RUN DOWN.

William Randolph Hearst, Progressive Press Advocacy

The popular magazines and newspapers added significant fuel to the progressive movement. They exaggerated descriptions of alleged dishonest conduct of Senators, causing intentional outrage in the public mind. President Theodore Roosevelt later described the writings as "yellow journalism." It was the term used for poorly researched, exaggerated, and sensational reporting.

William Randolph Hearst, was a Democrat U.S. House Representative from 1903-1907. His father had been a California U.S. Senator but lost his re-election to a Republican. It was similar to the story of William Jennings Bryan.

William Randolph Hearst's father, George Hearst owned the *San Francisco Examiner*.

William Randolph Hearst, (1863-1951)

William Randolph took over that paper in 1887 and also started the *Chicago Examiner*. In 1895 he took over the *New York Journal.* The competition with other New York papers started the "yellow journalism" period. William Randolph was a candidate in the New York City mayor and New York governor races. He lost those races and was the only Democrat to lose a New York state position in 1906. After that loss, he developed a dislike for both political parties. Hearst was believed to be one of the real people represented in the character of the movie *Citizen Kane.*[58]

William Randolph Hearst supported the Russian Revolution of 1917 and the Soviet State before changing his position years later.

Illustration, from *Harper's Weekly* cartoon of 1906 by W. A Rogers.

HEARST, THE WIZARD OF OOZE

[58] *Citizen Kane*, film Directed and produced by Orson Welles, 1941

President Andrew Johnson, Early advocate of "democratization" of the Constitution

President Andrew Johnson, the Democrat from Tennessee and former Vice President to Republican President Abraham Lincoln, filed two resolutions while serving in the U.S. House for direct election of senators in 1851 and 1852. As a Senator in 1860, he proposed the direct election to the Senate. As President in 1863, he again proposed direct election of Senators twice. His motivation was as a "scheme of democratic change." [59] He wanted to democratize the Constitution.

Senator Robert M Lafollette, Sr., Wisconsin

Robert Lafollette was a Republican U.S. Senator from Wisconsin from 1906 to 1925. He was previously a US. House Representative and Wisconsin State governor from 1901-1906. He was a graduate of University of Wisconsin and promoted social legislation by the universities to advise public policy for reforms. In 1904 Lafollette described his advocacy of social reform legislation in Wisconsin saying he "would never be content until it reaches every family in the State." He was one of the earliest advocates of direct election of Senators.

---

[59] Haynes, George, H. Election of Senators, 1906 p 102

Senator Robert M Lafollette Sr.

By 1910 Wisconsin led the nation in progressive reforms according to one political writer. "Wisconsin has carried democracy farther than any State save Oregon. "[60]

Lafollette led the *National Progressive Republican League*. Lafollette's fellow organizers included nine Republican Senators, six Republican governors, and thirteen U.S. House members. The object of the league was "to promote popular government and progressive legislation."[61]

The League President, Senator Bourne predicted the "advocates of popular government will get control of both Democrat and Republican parties."[62] Some questioned Lafollette's party affiliation. Frederic C Howe wrote "though a Republican, Lafollette is a

[60] Howe, Fredric Clemson, Wisconsin-An Experiment in Democracy, New York, Chas. Scribner's Sons, 1912, p. x

[61] Flower, B.O., Editor, *Twentieth Century Magazine* Vol 3 #18 p 546 March 1911

[62] Howe, Frederic C "What the National Progressive Republican League is Doing", *Lafollette's Magazine* Vol 3, April 8 1911 Madison, Wis. p9

Democrat with a small "d". His democracy is economic, industrial and social." [63]

Frederic C Howe, Political Scientist, Writer

The progressive political science academicians were active in the 1890's. Frederic C Howe was a PhD graduate of Johns Hopkins, and a Cleveland city councilman. He was later appointed as Commissioner of Immigration of the Port of New York. He later created a *National Progressive League* to support a Franklin D. Roosevelt presidency. He was a prolific writer for progressive publications.

Frederic Howe admired the German system and apparently disliked American government.

He wrote, "Political institutions in America have been designed on the principle of distrust. **Fear of people, fear of legislature, fear of the executive has inspired Constitution makers and law makers from the very beginning."[64]**

Howe criticized the "extreme rigidity in our federal and state constitutions. Amendment is made as

---

[63] Howe, Fredric Clemson, Wisconsin-An Experiment in Democracy, New York, Chas. Scribner's Sons, 1912, p 23

[64] Howe, Frederic C, The Constitution and Public Opinion, Academy of Political Science, 1914 p 7

difficult as possible."[65] He wrote this at a time when reformers had changed the State constitutions dozens of times. Some reformers wanted to change the Constitutions to eliminate State Senates and use the *initiative and referendum* system by the electorate.

Frederic Clemson Howe

Howe was inspired by the reforms in Germany based on scientific legislation. "Germany has identified science with politics more closely than has any other nation. **The State universities, technical and commercial colleges are consciously used for the advancement of the fatherland**. In Germany the

---

[65] Howe, Frederic C, <u>The Constitution and Public Opinion</u>, 1914, p 8

colleges are for the advancement of the fatherland."[66]

Howe praised Wisconsin and Germany for their embrace of progressivism and scientific legislation, **"Wisconsin is making the German idea her own."**[67] Howe also wrote, "Wisconsin is doing for America what Germany is doing for the world.[68]"

"Wisconsin has created a new profession, the profession of public service; it has adopted the German idea to American Soil"[69]

The *Wisconsin Idea* was a prototype for political scientists to experiment with social legislation. Howe gave special credit to the University of Wisconsin for the progressive changes. "The university has been the direct inspiration of many of the progressive laws of the past decade."[70]

Howe described the progressive "Wisconsin idea" as an experiment station in politics, in social and industrial legislation in the democratization of

---

[66] Howe, Fredric Clemson, Wisconsin-An Experiment in Democracy, 1912, New York, Chas. Scribner's Sons, p 38
[67] [67] Howe, Fredric Clemson, Wisconsin-An Experiment in Democracy, 1912, New York, Chas. Scribner's Sons, p 39
[68] [68] Howe, Fredric Clemson, Wisconsin-An Experiment in Democracy, 1912 New York, Chas. Scriber's Sons, p vii

[69] Howe, Fredric Clemson, Wisconsin-An Experiment in Democracy, 1912 New York, Chas. Scriber's Sons, p 46
[70] Howe, Fredric Clemson, Wisconsin-An Experiment in Democracy, 1912, New York, Chas. Scribner's Sons, p 40

science and higher education. "It was a statewide laboratory where popular government was tested on its reaction on people, distribution of wealth and social wellbeing. "[71]

Progressives were unhappy with the progress in America in spite of all the Constitutional changes. He stated," The American state is probably our most conspicuous political failure."[72]

He especially admired the success of the 1911 Wisconsin State income tax, "was a novel idea and only tried previously in 2-3 other States where it failed."[73]

Edward Alsworth Ross, Sociology Professor, Writer

Edward Alsworth Ross was a sociology professor at the University of Nebraska from 1900 to 1905 when he wrote Social Control, A Survey of the Foundations of Order.

[71] Howe, Fredric Clemson, Wisconsin-An Experiment in Democracy, New York, Chas. Scribner's Sons, 1912, p. vii

[72] Howe, Fredric Clemson, Wisconsin-An Experiment in Democracy, New York, Chas. Scribner's Sons, 1912, p. vii

[73] Howe, Fredric Clemson, Wisconsin-An Experiment in Democracy, 1912, New York, Chas. Scribner's Sons, p 42

In 1906, he moved to the University of Wisconsin where he wrote <u>Changing America, Studies in Contemporary Society.</u>

He dedicated the <u>Social Control</u> text to "my master, Lester F Ward".   Ward, a sociologist, has been called the *"Father of the Modern Welfare State."* Ross was related through marriage to Lester F Ward.

Edward Alsworth Ross

In 1892, Ross wrote "a group control of conduct is therefore just what we should look for." In contrast to the Founding Fathers, he exhibited the typical academic elitism of many progressives, "As higher education claiming more and more years of one's life widens the space between those who possess it and those who do not and as the enlightenment of the public, the learned castes and professions the mandarinate will infallibly draw to itself a greater and greater share of social power." [74]

In his book, <u>Changing America: Studies in Contemporary Society</u>[75], Ross disparaged Founders John Adams and Alexander Hamilton as elitists. He dedicated this book to Albion Small, a fellow progressive leader. Small attended the University of Berlin and began the first Department of Sociology in the U.S. He promoted legislation for "Social Betterment".

Ross wrote favorably about the socialist government of Milwaukee Wisconsin. Following the socialist election win in 1910. Milwaukee organized a *Bureau of Economy and Efficiency*, headed by Ross associate, John R. Commons from the University of Wisconsin.

In 1917, E.A. Ross visited Russia and endorsed the Russian Revolution. In 1940 he became the national chairman of the ACLU.

E A Ross and William Jennings Bryan were not the only progressives from Nebraska. Ross worked with Roscoe Pound at the University of Nebraska. Pound later became the Dean of Harvard Law School although he never finished law school but graduated

---

[74] Ross, Edward Alsworth, <u>Social Control A Survey of the Foundations of Order,</u> MacMillan, New York 1901 p88

[75] Ross, Edward Alsworth, <u>Changing America: Studies in Contemporary Society,</u> Chautauqua Press, Chautauqua New York, 1909, 1912, The Century Co., 1915 Chautauqua

as a botanist.   Roscoe Pound later wrote <u>Social Control Through Law</u>[76].   Pound and Ross both advocated social control of the citizens through government legislation.

Roscoe Pound, Dean of Harvard Law School

Roscoe Pound advanced a progressive ideology of sociological jurisprudence as Dean of Nebraska and Harvard Law Schools. Pound reflected the attitude of progressive leaders when he wrote, **"the legal system exhibits too great a respect for the individual and too little respect for the needs of society"**[77]

---

[76] Pound, Roscoe, <u>Social Control Through Law,</u> Yale University Press 1942

[77] Pound, Roscoe, <u>The Spirit of the Common Law</u>, 1921

Chapter Five

The Progressive Reformers Promises About the Amendment

Promise #1 It will do away with deadlocks, scandals and bribery.[78]

U.S. House Representative John Corliss repeated the propaganda in support of the Amendment. "We have gone through a veritable epidemic of investigations resulting from Senate elections and they have invariably resulted in exoneration. By popular vote a source of great temptation is removed, and the welfare of the people is made more secure. When you take from State legislatures this power of

---

[78] *The Chautauqua,* 67 105-7 July 1912

election you remove a large measure of corporate influence and corruption."[79]

Senator Jeff Davis, a Democrat from Arkansas, supported the Amendment on a foolish assumption, "With the direct vote of the people in the selection of senators these corrupt practices would be impossible." [80]

The reformers had no reason to assume there would be less corruption or special interest by direct election. In fact, the direct election of Senators made the Senate easier to influence through direct contact and the need for campaign capital.

There were ten times as many contested election cases in the House of Representatives. The greater number of contested elections in the popularly elected House should have revealed the false argument at the time. Corporate interests flourished in Washington DC after the removal of State legislature election of Senators.

Reformers said their Amendment would resolve the gridlocks in State legislatures on the election of Senators. However, only 2% of elections were tied in a deadlock. A number of Senate vacancies due to State legislature deadlocks began in 1893. Except

[79] U.S. Rep. John B Corliss, *The Times*, May 12 1898 p 4

[80] Senator Jeff Davis Congressional Record 46;1634-6 January 30 1911

for four vacancies in Delaware and one in Pennsylvania all remaining 11 vacancies occurred in the newer Western states. [81]

A list of vacancies due to deadlocks is in Appendix C

Promise #2   Less Corruption and Corporate Interests through Direct Election of Senators

The reformers believed the State legislatures were corrupted. "Take from the legislatures the selection of U.S. Senators and you will destroy the most potent power by which corporate influence now holds sway." [82] Corporate influence did not diminish.

Evident in the Congressional debates was a passionate and irrational hatred of the U.S. Senate. Democrat and progressive U.S. Rep. William Sulzer said, "We witness today in the personnel of the U.S. Senate the supplanting of representative democracy by representative plutocracy. Here is the last bulwark of the predatory few. Here is the citadel of the unscrupulous monopolies. And more and more the special interests of the country, realizing the importance of the Senate, are combining their forces

[81] Haynes, George H, The Election of Senators, 1906

[82] Mohn, Earl John, "*The Advisability of Electing U.S. Senators by Popular Ballot*, Georgetown Law School, 1909 p6

to control the election of Federal senators through their sinister influence in state legislatures." [83]

Sulzer was impeached from office as New York governor in 1913 but won election as a New York legislature representative for the Progressive Party.

History has revealed that special interest influence has been more efficient and responsive in the re-election campaigns of their favored candidates of both parties with direct election. The issues of the candidates have become more shallow and slick as well-funded mass marketing to voters. Statesmen without special interest funding cannot compete in the expenses of mass marketing to the public.

There has been increased corruption when the State legislatures no longer supervised the elections of Senators.

Promise #3 It will free the legislatures with time and opportunity to transact business instead of vote for senator.[84]

A newspaper report of 1896 from a committee promoting the Amendment said "the present system of electing Senators is the great length of time frequently consumed in the election and the

---

[83] U.S. Representative William Sulzer, Democrat, New York, Congressional Record 48 6802, May 13 1912 (archive.org p 71)

[84] Ibid

consequent distraction of the legislative minds from business-to say nothing of the strife ill feeling and contention that too often follow in the wake of such contests."[85]

An essay in a progressive monthly stated "This new method of electing senators would be very beneficial to the State legislatures. These are elected primarily to consider local and State affairs, and it is better that they should not be hampered with national obligations."[86]

If the editor was familiar with the *Federalist Papers* he would realize that it was entirely wrong from the perspective of the Founders. Election of U.S. Senators by the State legislatures insured that they could retain their sovereignty and control federal expansion.

Promise #4 It will eliminate bi partisan intrigues.[87]

The arguments between the progressives and constitutionalists expanded the divisions between and within Republican and Democrats. Both parties became mired in the increasing divisions. The

---

[85] *Evening Star*, March 20 1896 p. 11 Washington DC

[86] Fox, Charles James, *Arena*, 27; 455-67 May 1902 p 461 archive.org

[87] Ibid

Republicans embraced progressivism for only a decade.

Promise #5 It will make governing more efficient and responsible.[88]

The 17th Amendment succeeded in making legislation more efficient but that was contrary to the Founders intent. It has led to irresponsible laws just as the Founders predicted.

An essay in a progressive magazine in 1902 admitted, "The Senate should no doubt exercise a certain restraining influence over the House. Many different opinions have existed on this subject but today the only sound principle is that the Senate being elected for a longer term than the House and being composed of older and usually more prominent men, represents the more permanent interests of the nation which at certain moments are apt to be disregarded; while the House is more responsive to the momentary impulses of the people."[89]

In spite of the well-reasoned argument, the essay continued in support of the Amendment, "to claim that their acknowledged conservatism and dignity

---

[88] Ibid

[89] Fox, Charles James, *Arena*, 27;455-67 May 1902

are based solely or even principally upon their manner of election is ridiculous."[90]

History and statistics would prove the essay wrong a century later. Indirect election was critical to avoiding public passion and allowing the Senate to deliberate on popular issues.

Promise #6 It will make the Senate more responsive and progressive.[91]

The Senate was not supposed to be responsive to public passion. It was supposed to deliberate carefully.

The aggressiveness of reformers is displayed in an article in the *Evening Star,* "Public opinion, it is argued demands the change proposed; the demand is loud and emphatic; pronounced as it is imperative; earnest as it seems to be, almost unanimous among the great masses of the people."[92] The article continues "the tendency of public opinion, the report

---

[90] Fox, Charles James, *Arena,* May 1902 p 460

[91] Ibid "What are the benefits of the reform? It will do away with deadlocks, scandals, and the purchase of senator appointments. It will free the legislatures and give them more time and opportunity to transact business. It will eliminate bi partisan intrigues. It will make for greater efficiency and responsibility in state government. As to its effect on the Senate.... It is certain that the Senate as a whole will be more responsive and progressive. (Chautauqua 67:105-7 July 1912

[92] Evening Star, Washington DC March 20 1896, p11

concludes is to disparage the Senate and depreciate its dignity, its usefulness its integrity, its power. If there is any cause for this tendency in the public mind it should be removed without delay."

The public outrage had been driven by the reformers. Bryan recognized their success in driving the change, "Four years ago in its platform of 1908 the democratic party directed attention to the awakening then beginning to make itself felt, **declaring the spirit of progressivism that the party has faithfully cultivated and which is now dominant in the public thought** in these words "we rejoice at the increasing signs of an awakening throughout the country."[93]

Another Senator's support was based on a false promise, "It will greatly diminish the temptation to gerrymander senatorial and representative districts by State legislatures in the interest of the political party in control."[94]

History has revealed that State legislatures have continued to gerrymander legislative districts. The most significant impact has been the increased

---

[93] [93] Bryan, William Jennings, *The Commoner*, Editorial, October 18 1912 p 6

[94] Senator John H Mitchell, *Forum*, 21, ;385 June 1896 also, "Selected Articles", 1912, p 111

representation of urban areas due to the popular vote.

Promise #7 The Senate will no longer be a rich man's club[95]

This was typical propaganda against the Senate and it is false.

In 1892, of 88 senators there were six millionaires. 20 senators had incomes in excess of $300,000. Only four senators could be connected with corporate wealth and corporate interests. Four of nine senators could be classified as rank and file or government workers.[96]

Another writer defended the Senate, "The proportion of rich men in the Senate is not greater than that which exists in every State and Community in the whole country where the honest responsibility of public office is shared alike by the rich, comfortable and poor."[97]

A 1909 essay in support of the Amendment called them, "Oil Senators, "Steel Senators" and "Railroad Senators". The essay insisted "popular election, it

[95] Haynes, George H, Election of Senators, p 173

[96] Haynes, George H, Election of Senators, New York, Henry Holt, 1906

[97] Edmunds, George F, Senate Doc 25 54th Congress Nov 13 1890

may also be contended with force, would lessen the influence of wealth upon the Senate."[98]

History has revealed the cost of popular election campaigns has required special interest negotiations in both parties.

Illustration: A political cartoon from *Puck*, 1889, depicting the populist charge of alleged control of wealth in the Senate, "The Bosses of the Senate" by J. Keppler.

Promise #8 The reformers could improve the Constitution which is old and out of date

The reformers claimed, "the Constitution today differs in spirit if not in letter. Many opinions quite rational in 1787 would be ridiculous in 1912. The

[98] Haynes, George H. Election of Senators, 1906 p 172

political development of U.S. gradual change from aristocratic and conservative ideals of framers to popular democratic ideas of today."[99]

Another essay written in 1909 ignored the Founders' timeless goals of natural rights of men, "the advancement of political science, the astounding growth of our country and the intelligence of our people have removed the reason and this is proven by the fact that all over this land the trend seems to be towards a more popular government."[100]

The trend was for increased democratization of the country. Public passion for government programs generated by the progressives caused the trend. The effort was contrary to the Constitution. The Founders intended to create a government that could withstand popular passion and survive. The reformers limited the potential time span of our country, the individual liberties and the economic health.

The appeal for democracy was an easy argument when the Founders debates had been forgotten. "There are several sound and positive arguments for the election of senators by direct vote of the people. First among them is that this new method is the

[99] "Selected Articles on the Election of Senators", Minneapolis, edited C. E Fanning, 1912, p70

[100] Mohn, Earl John, "The Advisability of Electing U.S. Senators by Popular Ballot", Georgetown Law School. p 5

logical outcome of our political development, and is quite in accord with our ideals of government today. Every student of history knows that the political development of the U.S. has been a gradual change from the aristocratic and conservative ideals of the framers of our government to the popular democratic ideas of today."[101]

An author who presumed to write a rational and unbiased view of the proposed Amendment declared, "The Constitution has already been repeatedly amended without impairing the veneration in which it is held by the people."[102] He failed to realize before the progressive Amendments all but one of the 15 Amendments promoted individual and States rights over the federal government.

Promise #9 The progressive reformers believed the people would become better informed voters.

A news article declared, "Finally one important argument in favor of popular election is that it would be of great political value to the people themselves. The great store of political learning and experience which the railroads, telegraphs and newspapers have aided in placing before the people is not always

---

[101] Fox, Charles James, *Arena* 27; 455-67 May 1902

[102] Haynes, George H, Election of Senators, p 205

readily absorbed. There is no doubt that the people do not take entire advantage of their opportunities in this respect and it is equally undeniable that the government should do all it its power to encourage either directly or indirectly the acquisition of political knowledge and experience by the people, because on the political foresight and ability of the people depends absolutely the welfare of all democratic governments." [103]

A supporter of the Amendment claimed an advantage was the "voters would become better informed about political science because they were voting directly."[104] History has revealed the voters can be convinced to re-elect Senators based on marketing even with documented poor performance.

Their misguided suggestion was repeated by a political scientist, "This change in electing Senators would give the people much more powerful influence over the Federal government."[105]

History has proven this false. The voters have re-elected incumbents who have committed unethical practices, used their power for selfish goals and intimidated voters.

[103] Fox, Charles James, *Arena* 27 455-67 May 1902

[104] Haynes, George H, Election of Senators, p 209

[105] Mohn, Earl John "The Advisability of Electing US Senators by Popular Ballot", Georgetown Law School 1909, p 12

Chapter Six

The Reformers Failure to Understand Constitutional History

Constitutional History Failure #1 The Constitution was not well conceived.

James Madison wrote in *Federalist Paper* #14 in praise for the new innovative American Constitution for the private rights and public happiness, "marveled at the exactness and correctness of the document which had pursued a new and more noble course". He believed it had no parallel in human society.

The Founders knew they were creating a Constitution that was innovative to the world. It had no parallel in human history. They intended a new and noble cause for life, liberty and the pursuit of happiness unrestricted by tyranny of the royalty or the democratic mobs.

Constitutional History Failure #2 The Founding Fathers did not trust the people.

The Founders did not trust the government or political leaders. Senator George F Hoar answered their claim, "The authors of the *Declaration of Independence* trusted the people when they made those great declarations of natural rights. But they trusted them also with **as profound and implicit a trust when they submitted to them constitutions filled with restraints which alike secure minorities and individuals against injustice and oppression from majorities and secure the whole people against their own hasty and inconsiderate action...** It is not because the framers of our Constitution distrusted the people; it is because they trusted the people that they confidently asked their adoption of a Constitution which compelled them to deliberation to sober thought to delegated power to action through selected agencies and instrumentalities."[106]

The Founders had predicted the intent of mob democracies to force legislation and knew the democracy would limit the duration of our government. Restraining mob democracy was essential for individual and minority rights.

[106] Senator George F Hoar, Congressional Record, April 3 1893 25 101-110

Constitutional History Failure #3 The change would not deprive the States of their Constitutional sovereignty.

A news article declared without proof that the States would not be injured, "The objection is not tenable that any proposed change in the mode of electing senators can be properly regarded as an attempt to deprive the states, respectively as states in their sovereign or political capacity, of their legal representation in the Senate. It proposes a change in the mode—only this and nothing more- by which the states respectively and the people thereof shall choose their representatives in the Senate."[107]

The duty of the U.S. Senate was changed from representing the State legislatures to representing the people. The people will usually desire programs paid by the federal government on their behalf. The candidates for Senate will promise what the public desires. The logical assumption would be that if the legislatures did not vote for the Senator, the allegiances would change. It was difficult for Senators to resist the popular demands of progressive ideas. They were able to resist only if they were indirectly elected and represented the state governments.

It was not the role of the Senate to represent the popular will of the people. It was to resist the

---

[107] *Evening Star* Library of Congress, March 20 1896

passion of the moment and resist popular will. The U.S. House was already representing the popular will.

Constitution History Failure #4 Popular passion is justification for the amendment.

It was popular passion that the Founders intended to avoid. The Senate was designed to avoid popular passion legislation.

Alexander Hamilton made it clear in *Federalist #6 and #9* that America was not based on a democracy, but a commercial republic. The Senate would be a check on the passion on the public majority that might affect the liberties of the minority.

The Founding Fathers knew that a pure democracy would rule as a mob, forcing their will on the minority. The representative republic was designed to prevent the mob action on any individual.

Senator George F. Hoar was the mature statesman representing the Founders intent in opposing the Amendment. Hoar said, "There is but one road to the enjoyment of the confidence of the people and that is to counsel them to wise, honest, and safe policies. The public man who appeals to temporary opinion of who flatters temporary passion will find his hold upon power as temporary and short lived..."[108]

---

[108] Senator George F Hoar, Congressional Record, April 3 1893, 25 101-110

Constitutional History Failure #5 Constitutions can be amended when goals are unconstitutional

Oregon amended its Constitution 23 times between 1904 and 1910. In California 23 amendments occurred in 1911. In Ohio 34 changes occurred in 1913.

Thirty six revisions and fifty Constitutional changes to State Constitutions had already been made. The revised State Constitutions had already limited the role of State governments and legislatures. By the time of the ratification the State legislatures had been minimized and attacked in their role.

Surprisingly, over twenty individual States had voted already for an Article V Constitution Convention for direct election of Senators. Progressive State leaders had actively engaged in the movement to reduce their own influence.

By 1911, twenty two States had filed an application for an Article V Convention to amend the Constitution and give away their Constitutional power. A list of those States is in Appendix D.

Constitutional History Failure #6 The deliberation of a conservative Senate was not important

"Never before has there been proposed so far as I know, a change which is to affect the great balance of political power which our fathers adjusted with so much care."[109] Senator Hoar described the rush to reform.

"The House of Representatives without a debate has passed resolutions for submitting the change to the states. The **careless and thoughtless dealing with this subject is shown by the proposal to take from Congress all power over the manner of electing senators a step which would go far, in any judgment to change this country from a nation into a league or confederacy.** ...Although our constitutions, state and national are all in writing there are constant attempts to make changes of the most radical and vital character and to bring them about suddenly and without deliberation or discussion by popular action." [110]

Senator George F Hoar appealed for patience against the rush. "A present impatience is not only no good reason for making a change, but its existence seems to me an especial reason for postponing it."[111]

---

[109] George Hoar, Speech, Congressional Record, Senate Doc 232 59th Congress 1st session

[110] Senator George F Hoar, Congressional Record, 25 101-110 April 3 1893

[111] Senator George F Hoar, Congressional Record, April 3 1893 Record 25

Senator Hoar appealed for patience in spite of the uneasiness. "Schools, universities, church, law and private habits of the people... Complaint, impatience, uneasiness attend upon everything... They are the sign of vigorous health and if soberly and thoughtfully dealt with are the conditions of all life and growth."

Even Senator Hoar was affected by the propaganda war, "We must judge the Senate, as I have said by the experience of a century and not by a few recent failures"[112]

The progressives rushed the issue in the Senate through the direct threat of a Constitutional Convention that they threatened would include other progressive plans undesirable to conservatives and Constitutionalists.

Illustrations: Some of the historical official proposals for the direct election of Senators from the Senate archives

---

[112] [112] Senator George F Hoar, Congressional Record, April 3 1893 Record 25

H. Res. 39.

IN THE SENATE OF THE UNITED STATES.

MAY 15 1911

Referred to the ~~COMMITTEE~~ .... and
ordered to be printed, and lie on the table.

AMENDMENT

Intended to be proposed by Mr. Senator .... to the H. Res. 39)

Proposing an amendment to the Constitution providing that Senators shall be elected by the people of the several States.

Strike out all after the resolving clause and insert the following:

That in lieu of the first paragraph of section three of Article I of the Constitution of the United States, and in lieu of so much of paragraph two of the same section as relates to the filling of vacancies, the following be proposed as an amendment to the Constitution, which shall be valid to all intents and purposes as part of the Constitution when ratified by the legislatures of three-fourths of the States:

" The Senate of the United States shall be composed of two Senators from each State, elected by the people thereof, for six years; and each Senator shall have one vote. The electors in each State shall have the qualifications requisite for electors of the most numerous branch of the State legislatures.

" When vacancies happen in the representation of any State in the Senate, the executive authority of such State shall issue writs of election to fill such vacancies: Provided, That the legislature of any State may empower the executive thereof to make temporary appointments until the people fill the vacancies by election as the legislature may direct.

" This amendment shall not be so construed as to affect the election or term of any Senator chosen before it becomes valid as part of the Constitution."

State Grange of Illinois,

Patrons of Husbandry,

SECRETARY'S OFFICE.

Dunlap, Ill., _Jan 1_   1898.

At the 26th Annual Session of the Illinois State Grange, at Springfield Ills, Dec 14-16, 1897. The following was adopted.

Whereas. The United States Senate is largely composed of Millionaires, who frequently owe their election to the lavish expenditure of money;

Resolved. In order to make them more directly accountable to the people, they should be elected by popular vote.

Attest

Thos Keady. Sec

Chapter Seven

The Direct Democracy Reformers

The Founders were correct in forecasting the intent of factions to legislate against other citizens. The Founding Fathers of our Constitution understood that factions of citizens had undermined democracies and republics throughout history.

There were several distinct factions who promoted these progressive causes; direct election of senators, graduated income tax, prohibition and other reforms.

The factions were composed of; the academicians, the progressive press, the agrarian activists, the direct democracy advocates, the socialist advocates, and the partisan politicians.

This text has already discussed the motivation of the academic, progressive press and political reformers. A less obvious faction of reformers were the direct democracy activists. Included in their ranks were agrarian activists and socialists. The movement started in the western States.

The direct democracy legislation was proposed in Oregon in 1892, approved in South Dakota in 1898, Utah in 1900 and in Oregon in 1902. Between 1906 and 1918 sixteen more states promoted direct legislation.

Oregon's direct democracy movement was begun by William U'Ren. He was a progressive spiritualist who founded the *Direct Legislation League* and inspired the *Peoples Power League*. It was one of the most active progressive organizations, bringing together the agrarian activists and labor. They promoted unicameral government, (one legislative body), and elimination of Senates.

U'Ren was inspired by a book written by James William Sullivan, Direct Legislation by the Citizenship Through the Initiative and Referendum. The book included a chapter, "To Peaceful Revolution".[113]

Sullivan's intent was to change the government of the United States to advance direct democracy. Sullivan wrote accurately "there is a radical difference between a democracy and a representative government." He revealed his

---

[113] Sullivan, James W, Direct Legislation by the Citizenship Through the Initiative and Referendum, New York, Twentieth Century Publishing, 1892 {1848-1938}

contempt for representative government and desire for social reconstruction. "To radical reformers further encouragement must come with continued reflection on the importance to them of direct legislation... before any project of social reconstruction can be followed out to the end there stands a question antecedent to every other. It is the abolition of the lawmaking monopoly. Until that monopoly is ended no law favorable to the masses can be secure."[114]

Sullivan was influenced by the Swiss socialist, Karl Burkli, who wrote a similarly titled pamphlet thirty years earlier, *Direct Legislation by the People, versus Representative Government.* Burkli had started a utopian community in Texas in 1855.

It requires significant organizing effort to create popular majorities on special interests. The organized factions have greater power than the individual. The lobbying factions of special interests are far more equipped to create a voting majority than individual citizens. Organizations with time and resources were behind many Constitutional changes. If their needs were unconstitutional, they changed the constitutions.

---

[114] Sullivan, William, Direct Legislation by the Citizenship through the Initiative and Referendum, 1892 p 100

Chapter Eight

The Rush to Amend

Senator George F Hoar warned of the urgency behind the movement. "If the great reasons which moved our fathers to establish this chamber (Senate) ...to remove it from the operation of the fleeting passions of the hour, and to remove the appointment of the men who are to compose it as far as may be from the **temporary excitements which so often move the people to their own harm** are understood anywhere those reasons must be understood by the men who fill these seats" [115]

Democrat Senator Jeff Davis often spoke with contempt toward the majority and threatened public passion on unpopular votes. He said "we, upon the democratic side of this chamber, have warned the majority in this body repeatedly of **the terrible**

---

[115] Senator George F Hoar, Congressional Record 25 April 3 1893

cyclone of public indignation that awaited them should they ruthlessly and recklessly trample upon the rights of the people in the form of the present tariff law."[116]

A decade earlier, the senior Senators were still confident in 1893 of their position of carefully considering legislation. "It is marvelous to see how safe, conservative, and beneficent has been our national legislation in spite of all the violence and all the extreme utterances of the journals and the platforms."[117]

After a few years of continuous attack, the Senators confidence would disappear.

The Amendment proponents had contingency plans if needed. If the Senate selection by State legislatures did not accept their demise, there was an alternate plan. The progressives realized they could force the hand of the Senate to approve the Amendment resolution.

The progressives had begun a campaign for a Constitutional Convention of States, (Article V) to effect an amendment. William Jennings Bryan threatened even greater changes in the Constitution

---

[116] Senator Jeff Davis, Congressional Record, 46; 1634-6 January 30 1911

[117] Senator George F Hoar, Congressional Record, 25 101-110 April 3 1893

if a Convention for the direct election of senators was required. They had over twenty States already filing for an Amendment.

Jennings warned, "Upon the demand of thirty one States congress is bound to call a Constitutional Convention which might submit **amendments not only for income tax and popular elections of senators but for other things even less welcome to truly conservative members of the upper house.** It is not improbable that, if forced to choose between submitting an amendment for direct election of senators and calling a Constitutional Convention the Senate would accept the former. **We hope to see that choice forced upon it** and would cheerfully see the income tax matter deferred for that purpose."[118] It was a serious threat. A list of States requesting a convention for direct election of Senators is in the Appendix D.

The reformers had a third contingency plan. They could force the change through the ballot *initiative and referendum* already passed in many States. In Oregon, the campaign had begun. A newspaper reported "The issue at the coming election is whether the people of Oregon shall retreat in the battle for direct election of senators or go forward. A law has been initiated by the *People's Power League*

---

[118] Bryan, William Jennings, *The Commoner*, August 13 1909 p 6

that directs the legislature to ratify the choice of the people regardless of party."[119]

The existing Senate was clearly caught without a strategy or understanding of the depth of the opposition.

Even State legislators were caught up in the popular passion of progressive causes and apparently unconcerned about forfeiting their own control over the federal government.

Confidence in the proposed Amendment was declared in a newspaper article in 1906, "The present method of electing Senators is doomed. To bring about a reform will require time, but the Senate will yet be made responsive to the public will and the only way to bring about that desirable result is to make the Senators dependent for elections upon the vote of the people." [120]

By ratifying the Amendment the State legislatures abandoned their responsibility to a Constitutional Republic government. The timing was perfectly rushed for the progressives.

---

[119] *Daily Capital Journal* February 18 1908 p 2

[120] *Aberdeen Herald*, March 1 1906 p

Chapter Nine

The Progressive Propaganda

How they raised public passion against the Senate, Senators and against the original intent of the Constitutional Amendment

"Newspapers, railroads telegraphs and accumulated political experience have in the course of time become some of the main causes of this change."[121]

The attacks in the popular media started decades before the Seventeenth Amendment was proposed. An article in 1908 accurately described the atmosphere, "Have the lurid headlines of yellow journalism as to the treason of the senate the irresponsible utterances of those whose sorry role is

---

[121] Fox, Charles James, *Arena*, 27 455-67 May 1902

to pander to the morbid appetite for the sensational."[122]

Senator Porter J McCumber seemed to realize the political tactic of controlling national syndication of news. "There is also another dangerous portion of the press and which must be reckoned with. It is that portion which, having a view of its own upon economic questions, seeks to destroy by unfair publications any public official who does not conform to its views. This is one of the greatest dangers to our people to day demoralizing alike to the corruptly inclined and misleading to those who are ignorant of the real questions involved."[123]

He warned of the effect of the negative writings, "A falsehood in print looks exactly like the truth to the man who does not know it is a falsehood and hence the temptation to use this weapon of political warfare in a campaign before the public. He added that the press weapon would be more effective on the uninformed public than on an informed State legislator, "a weapon which is abandoned as practically useless in a campaign before.... The better informed ... more easily informed members of the legislatures. "[124]

[122] O'Neal, Emmet, *North American Review*, 188; 700-15 Nov 1908

[123] Senator Porter J McCumber, Congressional Record 47 1879-84 June 12 1911

[124] Senator Porter J McCumber, Congressional Record 47- 1879-84 June 12 1911

Major public propaganda for the Amendment was distributed in two separate national magazine publications in 1906 and 1911.

Treason of the Senate, 1906

In 1905, William Randolph Hearst an Amendment supporter, started *Cosmopolitan* magazine. In 1906

he hired David Graham Phillips to write a series of nine articles, "Treason of the Senate". Phillips was better known for his fictional stories. It was this sensational series that created the immediate impression in the public that the U.S. Senate was a failure and had to be changed.

Many believe that the series by Phillips was responsible for the passage of the 17th Amendment.

The 1906 series of nine articles, *Treason of the Senate,* was filled with insults toward 21 Senators, 18 Republicans and 3 Democrats. Phillips employed his creative writing skills to frame the Senators as hideous characters. It is not surprising the public responded with a passion to change the Senate.

The Editorial foreword indicates intent. The following are excerpts of the foreword, "The editor trusts that... the ultimate gratification of the outraged public in seeing its misrepresentatives scotched by the hand of that artist in exposure who has undertaken the worthy task of writing this, the most remarkable story of political corruption ever told in print... For though Mr. Depew may leave the Senate chamber forever, his odor will remain."[125]

The following are excerpts of Phillips writing in the series,

"These committees carry on their colorless routine and their real work-promoting thievish legislation, preventing decent legislation devising ways and means of making rottenest dishonesty look like honesty and patriotism- these committees carry on their work in secrecy."[126]

In the following excerpt, Phillips speaks of the President of the Senate, Nelson Aldrich. "Has Aldrich intellect? Perhaps But he does not show it. He has

---

[125] Editor, *Cosmopolitan* Magazine, "Treason of the Senate", p 57 Phillips, David Graham, Quadrangle books, Chicago 1964 edited with introduction by George E Mowry and Judson A Grenier, Author's Note: from reprinted text, the magazine editor is not identified by name, the owner of the *Cosmopolitan* magazine was William Randolph Hearst.

[126] "Treason of the Senate", p 57 Phillips, David Graham, Quadrangle books, Chicago 1964 edited with introduction by George E Mowry and Judson A Grenier, p 93

never in his 25 years of service in the Senate introduced or advocated a measure that shows any conception of life above which might be expected of Hungry Joe. No, intellect is not the characteristic of Aldrich- or only of these traitors, or of the men they serve. A scurvy lot they are and they not with their smirking..."[127]

David Graham Phillips, the writer of the series, never witnessed the result of his work. He was shot in New York in 1911. It was not the powerful and wealthy men that he targeted in his article who were responsible. It was a mentally ill man that thought a fictional novel Phillips wrote was about his sister.

Phillips may have revealed his personal feeling about his writings in the preface of a fictional book he wrote in 1908, "The authors who know they were lying sank almost as low as the nasty-nice purveyor of false idealism and candied pruriency who fancied they were writing the truth."[128]

After his murder, Phillips was remembered in a memorial article as a devotee of Karl Marx. According to the article, Phillips had told the writer, "I spent most of my time reading Karl Marx's Das

---

[127] Phillips, David Graham, "Treason of the Senate", Cosmopolitan Magazine, Second Part, Nelson Aldrich, March to Nov 1906, (in Treason of the Senate, reprinted text, edited with introduction by George E Mowry and Judson A Grenier p 96,)

[128] Phillips, David Graham, Susan Lennox; Her Fall and Rise, New York, D. Appleton Co., 1917, published after his death, (preface by author written in 1908)

Kapital[129]. It is one of the most wonderful books I ever read. The lives and work of such men as Marx give us courage to fight against the growing reaction and the corrupt commercial conditions that threaten the very life of free government."[130]

Senator Joseph W Bailey, was one of three Democrats targeted. The article quoted Bailey, "But I insist, that such legislation belongs to the States and not to the general government."[131] Bailey was strictly defending the Constitution and this was a negative in the minds of reformers.

Bailey resigned from the Senate and he was the only Senator to officially argue the charges against him in the article. He concluded, "I want also to say to the country that the very fact that these attacks are permitted to pass unchallenged encourages men to make them. They misstate the record. They suppress the truth. Why? Because they feel that the men whom they attack will sit silent under their misrepresenations."[132]

How the Constitution Bars Democracy, 1911

[129] Marx, Karl, Das Kapital, Germany, Verlag von Otto Meisner, 1867

[130] Flower, B.O., "David Graham Phillips", Twentieth Century Magazine p 547-548

[131] Senator Bailey, Joseph W., quoted in Treason of the Senate, Cosmopolitan Magazine, Chapter "Bailey, The Patriot."

[132] Senator Bailey, Joseph W., Congressional Record, 59th Congress, 1st Session, Vol XL Senate

Another magazine article criticized the American Constitution directly. "How the Constitution Bars Democracy" was written by Robert Wickliffe Woolley, a progressive, a partisan Democrat and future Woodrow Wilson political appointee. He used the article to attack Republican Senators for blocking federal legislation and appointments of progressives.

The soft and circular propaganda used by the progressives are fully on display in the article *"How the Constitution Bars Democracy" by* Robert Wickliffe Woolley[133] (pictured above)

The *Pearson's Magazine* article begins with a raging partisan attack against Republicans, "Yet the oligarchy, which started in 1861 and has been practically self-perpetuating ever since, with the exception of the two years, 1893-1895, when

[133] Woolley, Robert Wickliffe, "How the Constitution Bars Democracy", Pearson's *Magazine* , New York, Pearson Publishing Co., Vol 25 No. 2, Feb. 1911

democrats and populists combines made a bare majority over the republicans, bids fair to continue to hold the people by the throat for an indefinite period in spite of the fact that the democrats have cut down the republican majority in the 62 Congress to eight."[134]

Wickliffe was later a Democrat political appointee to the U.S. Mint and ICC during President Woodrow Wilson's administration. He was the head of public relations for Wilson's re-election campaign.

The article *How the Constitution Bars Democracy* cleverly misrepresents positive attributes as negative. In some points the facts are misinterpreted. The entire premise of the article that the goal of the Founders was Democracy is incorrect. The following are examples of propaganda in the article.

Propaganda #1

"When the framers of the Constitution started to work on that historic instrument, they never intended to give equal representation to the States in the Senate."[135]

Robert Wickliffe Woolley, Pearson's Magazine p 220

---

[134] Woolley, Robert Wickliffe, "How the Constitution Bars Democracy", *Pearson's Magazine., Vol 25 # 2 Febr 1911*

[135] *Pearson's Magazine* p 220

This is incorrect based on the record. In *Federalist* #18 Alexander Hamilton used the Greek republic States as an example. The members retained independent and sovereign States. They had equal votes in the federal council. The Senate had the sole, exclusive right of war and peace, ambassadors, treaties and appointing judges.

In *Federalist* #18 Alexander Hamilton explained "the Greek states were similar to the U.S. The members retained independent and sovereign states with equal votes in the federal council. The Senate had sole, exclusive rights of war and peace, ambassadors, treaties and appointing judges."

Equal representation of independent States through the legislatures was a critical control on the potential for tyranny of the federal government.

Propaganda #2

"The Senate was created in a day when the rights of the aristocrat and his property were held to be above the rights of the ordinary human being."[136]

Robert Wickliffe Woolley, Pearson's Magazine p 221

The writer failed to acknowledge that all citizens deserve property rights. The Founders were concerned with protection of property and

---

[136] *Pearson's Magazine* ,p 221

individual rights. A mob democracy could be as injurious to freedom as a monarchy. The Founders protected liberty in the face of a popular majority that may take liberty for granted and make a public assault on private property rights.

James Madison wrote in *Federalist #10* about the diversity of citizens who all share property rights. He wrote "the diversity in the faculties of men from which the rights of property originate...Protection of different and unequal faculties acquiring property, possession of different degrees and kinds of property and division of society. It is propensity of mankind to fall into mutual animosities of those who hold and those without property."

Propaganda #3

It has long since been acknowledged that in the Senate the voice of the people is regarded as a secondary consideration [137]

Robert Wickliffe Woolley, Pearson's Magazine p 210

The writer failed to recognize the intentional restraint on popular passion by majorities against the minorities.

Founder Hamilton wrote in *Federalist Paper #27* "through the State legislatures a select body of men

---

[137] *Pearson's Magazine* p 221

would appoint members of the national Senate. These men would have peculiar care and judgment greater knowledge and more extensive information and less apt to be tainted by the spirit of faction and more out of reach of occasional ill-humors or temporary prejudices and propensities."

Propaganda #4

Political writers have penned volumes on the debauchery, so called of State legislatures and they seem to believe that the whole trouble will be cured when the Senators are chosen by direct vote."[138]

Robert Wickliffe Woolley, Pearson's Magazine p 221

The State legislatures had already been the subject of attack by progressives. The State Constitutions were amended fifty times through progressive demands. The progressives were experimenting with the mass democracy movement in the newer States. Elimination of Senates was a goal of some activists.

Propaganda #5

The proposed Amendment should take ideas presented by Bryan in 1896 as to making the

[138] *Pearson's Magazine* p 221

Senate more harmonious with the theory of popular government and more responsive to the fluctuations of public sentiment.[139]

Robert Wickliffe Woolley, Pearson's Magazine p 222

The Constitution was not intended to create a popular government but a representative government. In the original Senate, the Senators were answerable to the State legislature and could be withdrawn if they did not represent the States. Before the 17th Amendment, the state legislatures could have changed the method of election if the senators did not defend the States from federal overreach.

The Amendment did not conform to public sentiment, half of the States already allowed the people to vote directly for the Senator. The 17th Amendment forced it on all the State legislatures as a permanent device to remove State control. If the citizens of a State wanted to popularly elect a Senator, the Constitution did not forbid the ability. The State legislature was allowed to appoint based on their own method.

Propaganda #6

"Remember that the Constitution was made one hundred and twenty three years ago."[140]

---

[139] *Pearson's Magazine* p 222

The ideals of basic rights were as important now as then. The Founding Fathers based the Constitution on timeless ideals of individual liberty and the human condition and the experience of world governments over thousands of years. Socrates first wrote about the rights of life, liberty, and pursuit of happiness. Leaders were limited in their abuse of the citizens in 1215 in the *Magna Carta* and 1689 in the *Declaration of Rights*. The founders established the Constitution on the foundation of natural rights of life, liberty and happiness and freedoms.

The progressive ideas did not conform to individual liberty and they had to amend the Constitution to achieve their arrogant scientific legislation vision.

Propaganda #7

The leaders were by no means in favor of entrusting too much to the people.

The Founding Fathers designed a balanced and fair system. The design was to protect individual rights from factions of majorities. In *Federalist Paper* #51 James Madison explained the Senate and House would have different modes of election, a divided legislature, and little connection. The Senate had power from the States, the House from the people. It

---

was planned for a mixed character, individual delegations, distinct and co-equal. He explained the importance in a republic to guard against oppression of rulers and injustice of another part. Abuse of other factions can be targeted toward the rich or the poor.

Propaganda #8

The contest between the States was fast and furious and the final result not of more deliberation and wise counsel but compromise ...the Constitution.

Robert Wickliffe Woolley, Pearson's Magazine p 220

This is an insult on the Founders who worked for four months in stifling heat with the windows closed for privacy and wearing formal suits in respect. They ignored their health and comfort for the importance of the document for the people and the States.

James Madison in *Federalist Paper* #14 revealed his extreme confidence in a well-conceived document by his comments, "Marvel at the exactness and correctness. ... "pursued a new and more noble cause of private rights and public happiness. ...had accomplished a revolution with no parallel in human society."

Propaganda #9

Alexander Hamilton delivered his only speech in opposition to the plan to have States fully represented in the Senate.

This is another misleading statement. The *Federalist Paper* #17 Alexander Hamilton stated "If wantonness and lust of domination (federal jurisdiction) then the constituent body of national representative's people of the States would control the indulgence of an extravagant appetite."

Hamilton was clearly supportive of the State representation in Washington to prevent federal expansion.

Propaganda #10

Many students and writers believe the Senate is an entirely superfluous body and we could legislate quickly and effectively with one House and the President. It would give us a government of the people, by the people and for the people.

Robert Wickliffe Woolley, Pearson's Magazine p 220

The direct democracy activists and socialists promoted elimination of the Senate. The Founders did not intend to create a direct democracy. Senator George Hoar addressed this issue thoroughly in 1893. "Our founders wished to secure a dual legislative assembly. Every act of the legislature was to be twice considered and have the approbation of two different, separate houses. These two houses where to have different constituency, every proposed law must run the gauntlet of two diverse interests and be judged from at least two points of view. Third, the Senate was to represent equality of the States. Fourth, the Senate was to represent deliberation in the expression of the popular will by the length of the term of office and by its removal from the direct popular vote in the method of choice. It is this point at which the Senate is now attacked." [141]

Propaganda #11

In this country the Senate, contrary to the intentions of our forefathers, who thought they were following closely the idea of the House of Lords in creating the Senate, the upper house of Congress is kept in check only by the limitations of the Constitution. [142]

Robert Wickliffe Woolley, Pearson's Magazine p 220

This is another misleading statement. Alexander Hamilton wrote in *Federalist Paper* #28 '"Power being almost always the rival of power, the general government will at all times stand ready to check the usurpations of the State governments and these will have the same disposition toward the general government. The State governments afford security against invasion of liberty by the national authorities.

[141] Senator George F Hoar Congressional Record April 3 1893

[142] *Pearson's* p 220

The Political Scandal

In addition to the two major magazine articles already discussed, an unrelenting newspaper commentary was given to one Senatorial election. This election case was merged with the interests of the direct election of Senators. The stories undermined the confidence in the Senate.

Senator Weldon B Heyburn defended the record of honesty of Senate elections with statistics. He said, "The result is that the number of elections the legality of which was considered by the *Committee on Privileges and Elections,* from 1789 to 1903 was 101 cases. (out of 1,180) The number of Senators denied a seat in the Senate is 7. Seven out of 1,180 elected to the Senate in the lifetime of the government.   Where in the world or in the history of the world have the people shown such accuracy and judgment in the estimation of men and of their qualifications as is shown by that record?"[143]

Senator William Lorimer

In 1910 William Lorimer, a self-educated immigrant from England and brick merchant, was elected to the Senate by the Illinois legislature after a deadlock battle. The *Chicago Tribune* alleged that he had obtained his seat through bribery and corruption.

---

[143] Senator Heyburn, Weldon B, Congressional Record, Feb. 17 1911

Lorimer claimed innocence and asked the Senate to investigate the charges against him.

The majority report in the Senate cleared Lorimer after no claims of bribery were admitted. One member of the investigating committee did not agree and wrote a minority report. The progressive media raised the minority report as proof. Even after a year of scandal mongering stories by the progressive media, the Senate refused to invalidate the election.

Robert M Lafollette the Republican progressive leader from Wisconsin, urged the Senate to reopen the Lorimer case. A special committee of the Senate was formed to conduct a second investigation. After 180 witnesses and volumes of testimony the majority committee again stated it had failed to find any evidence of bribery or corrupt practices.

The minority report again demanded Lorimer's election be ruled invalid. They did however, admit he was not involved himself in the alleged acts by others. He was thrown out of the Senate due to public outcry. Lorimer returned to Chicago to a loyal fan base, but was unsuccessful in popular elections in 1916 and 1918.

The media attached the alleged scandal to the proposed Amendment. A gloating news article attempted to draw the connection for the voters, "The case with its record of sordid politics spread in glaring nakedness before the people will augment the already insistent demand that the control of senatorial election be taken from the hands of the legislature and vested in the sovereign power of the republic. The Lorimer case is a practical demonstration demanding that a system proved wrong, be ignited. The case seems to recognize the concern and attention to alleged dishonesty by two separate investigations of the same manner."[144]

[144] Daily Capital Journal, Oregon, "All Obstacle to Reform Become Stepping Stones To Its Accomplishment, "March 6 1911

Chapter Ten

The Outcome of the Seventeenth Amendment

Political Impact

The original U.S. Senate was appointed by the State legislatures. The candidates did not have to win popular appeal for election. They did not promise programs or special interest for campaign donations and votes from the public. Their responsibility was to the State legislatures to contain the federal government.

The popular elections increased special interests ability to impact the elections because of the increased cost of mass marketing. The special interests have a stake in incumbents winning elections to retain their ongoing influence. In 2010, 84% of incumbent Senators were re-elected. Special interests work effectively and directly with the

Senators and assist in personal election campaigns without the intervention of the State legislatures. It is far easier for the special interests to work directly than through the State legislatures.

In spite of the obvious failure of the amendment to deliver any of the expected promises, Delaware, Maryland, Rhode Island and Alabama State legislatures have ratified the 17th Amendment in recent years. Delaware failed to approve it in 1913.

In recent years Montana, Arizona, and Georgia State legislatures, apparently more aware of history, have made attempts to repeal the 17th Amendment.

The Economic Impact

Over decades, the most obvious evaluation of the impact of the Amendment is on tax and spending. The effects of the Amendment were not immediately observed after it was ratified. The progressives lost the elections in 1919. After prohibition, the public paid closer attention to government policies. A more conservative Congress opposed progressive reforms for a decade. During the administration of Franklin D Roosevelt the progressive reformers returned to power and controlled the New Deal programs.

Spending Impact

In 1910 the federal government spent $694 million. By 1922, federal spending was four times the federal spending in 1913. It again quadrupled by 1940. It again quadrupled by 1944 and despite the end of the war, never returned to below 1944 levels, but continued to grow. In 1980 the nearly continuous increase of federal spending reached $590,947 million.

In 1900 the federal government expenditures were less than 3% of GDP, where it had remained since the country's founding. By 2012, federal expenses were 24% of GDP, eight times higher. (Gross Domestic Product, a standard measure of our economy)

State and local costs were always twice as high as the federal costs before the 17th Amendment. By 1940 receipts and expenses of the federal government exceeded the State and local governments.

Now, the federal government has expanded to ten times the cost of State and local governments.

Cost Per Capita of Federal Government

In 1912 the cost of the federal government was $9 per capita. In 1932 the cost per capita was $31. In 1927 it was about $400. The federal spending gained momentum after WWII and the expansion of federal bureaucracy.

In 1950, $3,000 per capita was spent, and in 1960, $5,000. The dramatic rise continued predictably to

$6,000 in the 1970, $8,000 in 1980-1990 and now hovers around $11,000.

Debt Impact

In the forty years between 1930 and 1970 the federal government produced a **surplus** in only four years. In the forty years, 1818 to 1858 the federal government only had a **deficit** for four years.

The fiscal management of our nation was significantly better in the first 120 years, than in the last 100 years. Our politicians have accepted annual debt as standard in their attempt to win the popular vote in both houses. A list of annual Federal Debt as a % of GDP is in Appendix G.

Federal Bureaucracy

There are now over 2,000 federal agencies and bureaus with about 3 million federal employees. Most have been spawned by "parent" federal departments and agencies.

The State Department and Treasury were established in 1789. The Department of Justice, Interior, Agriculture and Commerce were also already in existence before the 17th Amendment.

In 1913, the Federal Reserve and Department of Labor were established. In 1953 the Health and Human Services was established with a universal mission, "to enhance and protect the health and well-being of all Americans." In 1965 the Department of Housing and Urban Development was founded and provided an avenue of federal tax investment in real estate. Their mission is described as using housing as a platform to improve quality of life. In 1966 the Department of Transportation was established. In 1967 the Department of Energy was created. In 1979 the Department of Education was established with a goal "to promote student achievement and global competitiveness".   In 1987 the Veterans Administration was established. In 1990 the Environmental Protection Agency was founded and in 2002, the Homeland Security Administration.

Federal agencies that are independent of the executive branch have added to the list, CIA, FCC, FEC, FTC, GSA, NLRB, NRC, SSA, and SBA.

Taxation Impact

Since 1915 the federal government has adjusted the tax brackets repeatedly. The federal income tax was initially marketed on the basis that it would never tax the income needed for daily living and the richest would pay only 7%. Within two years, the brackets and rates had changed.

The Federal Takeover

The States were not only removed from control over the federal expansion but they were now dependent on federal grant money to carry out the demands of the growing federal legislation.

The State legislatures became less important as the federal government began controlling issues previously undertaken by the States. The States became puppets for the federal government.

The U. S. Senators became free to ignore their own State legislatures. Some Senators even oppose the State government limits of federal power and voted for federal expansion. The Senate has confirmed appointments of Supreme Court Justices who were known to dismiss the sovereignty of States and overturn State laws. The power of States has further eroded after court decisions of those Justices.

The Impact on American Citizens

The federal bureaucracy and its growing budget has created departments and agencies never imagined by our Founding Fathers. Federal bureaucrats now intervene in ordinary decisions, such as; how American children are raised and taught, which appliances, light bulbs or cars are acceptable for purchase, and who we must rent our apartment or bake a cake in our private business. There is no longer private business rights or property rights that the federal bureaucracy cannot undermine for the benefit of society at large. This is exactly the tyranny that the Founding Fathers intended to avoid in their carefully constructed Constitution that protected the individual from the mobs and the tyrants. This is exactly the goal that some of the progressive reformers intended when they conceived the 17th Amendment. The State legislature appointed Senators was the critical balance to prevent federal over reach. Our economy and our individual rights cannot be protected from tyranny without the restoration of the State legislature controlled Senators.

The Partisan Political Outcome

The political advantage did not immediately become apparent. The Democrats lost the majority in 1919 and for thirteen years the Republicans held a significant majority of seats in Congress.

The Democrats won elections again during the depression and retained control of Washington DC for two generations.

With the 16th and 17th Amendments ratified, the federal treasury was used for a wide range of popular passions and to enhance political advantage to the majority of voters.

The Potential Nightmare

As the mob majorities assume greater political power and government control, some scenarios are predictable. There will be more federal interference and fewer individual rights. The federal government will decide who is entitled to enhanced rights based on public passions.

In the interest of social welfare, deeply held personal beliefs and personal moral codes will need to conform to the government policy. The legal rights of churches to preach messages from the Bible that are not in line with the government are already in debate. In past decades, churches in China hid themselves in secret "house churches". The future of America will produce the same persecution of churches who refuse to comply with government accepted messages. This was the real intent of separation of church from State. It was to keep the government out of the churches.

Compulsory equality of income through taxation and subsidies will be demanded by popular passion. A maximum income will be established for households to participate in any government program.

Property taxes will increase because income taxes are inadequate to pay for promised programs. The properties will inevitably be confiscated in the tax lien and tax deed system by the government or investors. Home ownership will be replaced by rentals through the government or large investment groups.

In the interest of fairness and efficiency, the government will decide which students are qualified for advanced training for professional occupations. Those decisions will be based on the decisions of officials based on bureaucratic standards. The framework for occupation directed education has already been established. In the former Soviet Union local communist leaders chose the children for academic opportunities. In the interest of leveling opportunity, parents will not be able to homeschool their children.

These nightmares of the Founders were the dreams of progressive reformers a century ago. The progressive dreams are now our reality. It is just as the Founders predicted.

Chapter Eleven

What Can Be Done

An internet search reveals many organizations that have joined in the effort to repeal the 17th Amendment. These organizations would welcome contributions and volunteers for the cause. Readers are encouraged to educate their family and friends. A simple bumper sticker can promote the cause to the public.

Mark R. Levin has written, <u>The Liberty Amendments, Restoring the American Republic</u>[145]. It is about the opportunity to change the Constitution through the State convention process. Levin suggests a number of amendments that could be proposed through the States, instead of Washington DC. Chapter Three of

---

[145] Levin, Mark R., <u>The Liberty Amendments, Restoring the American Republic</u>, New York, Threshold Editions, 2013

his book is titled, "An Amendment to Restore the Senate." The chapter offers a basic text of a repeal amendment and a discussion of the Seventeenth Amendment. Levin writes accurately, "State sovereignty exists mostly at the will of the federal government."

Levin provides the reader with an appreciation of the Constitution and describes the Article V Convention process.

Federalist #85 describes the reasoning and authority behind the amendment process.

The Founders accurately predicted that the States and the citizens would one day have to amend the Constitution to protect themselves from a tyrannical federal government.

The standard method of changing the Constitution through the Congress has been attempted 27 times. There have been two attempts of an Article V State Convention method from the States. It was attempted in 1861 before the Civil War and might have prevented the war. It was initiated by the reformers in 1911 to force the issue of the Seventeenth Amendment.

The necessity of repealing this Amendment is apparent to a broad base of libertarians, conservatives, Republicans and Democrats. In 2004, Zell Miller, a Democrat U S Senator spoke on repealing the 17th Amendment. The following are excerpts from his speech,

"Direct elections of senators, as good as that sounds, allowed Washington's special interests to call the shots, whether its filing judicial vacancies or issuing regulations. The State governments aided in their own collective suicide by going along with the popular fad of the time."

"The election of U.S. senators by the State legislatures was the linchpin that guaranteed the interests of the States would be protected. Today, State governments have to stand in line. They are just another one of many, many special interests that try to get senators to listen to them."

"That is exactly what happened in 1913 when the State legislatures, except for Utah and Delaware, rushed pell-mell to ratify the popular 17th amendment and by doing so, slashed their own throats and destroyed federalism forever. It was a victory for special interest tyranny and a blow to the power of State governments that would cripple them forever."

"The Amendment was a death of the careful balance between State and federal governments as designed by that brilliant and practical group of Founding Fathers, the two governments would be in competition with each other and neither could abuse or threaten the other. The balance created the two governments in competition so neither could cause abuse. Now. The special interests call the shots. State governments were crippled forever." [146]

[146] Senator Zell Miller, Speech, April 28 2004

Appendix A

The Historical Timeline

1826 U.S. House Rep. Henry R Storrs proposed an amendment for popular election of Senators on a hand written note.

1851, 1852 U.S. Rep Andrew Johnson, future President, proposed House Resolution for Direct Election of Senators.

1860 Senator Andrew Johnson, future President, proposes Senate proposal for Direct Election of Senators.

1868 President Andrew Johnson proposed an amendment for popular election of Senators and said no explanation was necessary. He is said to believe in the democratizing the Constitution.

1887 The State Grange of Illinois petitions for direct election of Senators. They repeat the request in 1898. It is hand written.

1892- The Populist Party proposed direct election of senators in its platform.

1893- The U.S. House had two-thirds vote for a direct election of the Senate.

1897 Utah passes a resolution for a State Convention to consider an Amendment.

1900 Direct Election of Senators is included in Democrat Party plank. Also included in 1904 and 1908.

1901 Colorado passes a resolution for a State Convention to consider an amendment.

1906 - The *Treason of the Senate* series is published by Cosmopolitan publisher William Randolph Hearst. .

1906 Iowa governor hosts a conference for all States in Des Moines promoting direct election of Senators.

1907 Louisiana passes a resolution for a State Convention to consider an amendment.

1907- The Senate is controlled by the Republicans as it has for decades at a two to one majority over Democrats. Proposals by the House for direct election of the Senate died in 1900, 1904 and 1908.

1908 Oregon passed the first law basing the selection of U.S. Senators in the State on a popular vote. Nebraska followed. There were already ten States with non-binding primaries.

1910- 31 State legislatures passed motions calling for reform of the Senate. Twenty seven States proposed an Article V Convention. Some States were using primary elections for the people to choose their Senators; some were binding on the legislature.

1910- 10 incoming Democrats are elected by the States. Fourteen of the thirty newly elected Senators had been elected through party primaries. In addition 8 Republican progressives join the Democrats to undermine the conservative leadership in the Senate. Ten Republican Senators who opposed reforms were voted out of office in the States with elections.

1911- The progressive Republicans joined Democrats against the election of the incoming chairman. The Republican Senators had controlled the Senate for the past 15 years opposed the Amendment.

1911- Former President Theodore Roosevelt approved the platform of the National Republican League including the Amendment. "Progressives Get a Boost From T R" reported January 26 1911 The Tacoma Times.

1911 The National Progressive Republican League issued a statement in support of the direct election of Senators. The executive committee was attended by Senators Bristow, Bourne, and Clapp. The Washington Times, Feb. 6 1911 "Progressives Ask Aid of Country in Direct Vote Fight

1911 The *House Joint Resolution 39* was sent to the Senate. It included a race rider that would have prevented federal supervision of elections. It was amended by the Senate to remove the race rider. A New York Times article reported "Up to 1911, attempts to amend the Constitution failed through the steady refusal of the Senate to pass resolutions. The House has passed the proposed amendment on July 1 1894, May 11 1898, April 13 1900, and Feb. 13 1902. In each case the Senate refused to concur. In the sixty-first Congress Senators Borah and Bristow forced the question to the front. On January 11 1911 Senator Borah was directed by the Senate Judiciary Committee to report his resolution." Reported in Chautauqua 67:105-7 July 1912

1912 A proposal was approved by the Senate on April 12, 1912 and by the House. The joint resolution was signed on May 13 1912.

1913 The Amendment was rejected by Utah and Delaware but approved by 36 States out of 48 total States.

1913 William Jennings Bryan declared the Seventeenth Amendment ratified on May 31 1913.

1916- The Republicans controlled State legislatures and would have controlled the Senate but with the Seventeenth Amendment, Democrat Senators were elected by popular vote.

Eighty years later...

1996 Arizona considered a resolution to repeal the 17th Amendment.

2002- Alabama ratified the Amendment, 89 years late.

2003 Montana considered a proposal to repeal the 17th Amendment It was defeated 9-40.

2010- Delaware approved the Seventeenth Amendment, 97 years after the Amendment was ratified. Delaware had initially rejected the Amendment.

2012- Maryland approved the Amendment, 99 years after it was ratified.

New Hampshire considered a resolution to repeal the Amendment. Tennessee considered a resolution to repeal. [147]

---

[147] Reported as news.

2013 Georgia considered a proposal to repeal the Seventeenth Amendment.

2014- Rhode Island approved the 17th Amendment

Appendix B

The Federal Deficits and Surpluses By Year

U.S. Census Bureau, 1789-1907

Year	Federal Expenses	(Deficit) /Surplus+
1791	$3,134,150	
1792	8,324,400	
1793	3,918,970	(805,995)
1796	7,427,494	(1,195,066)
1797	6,158,741	2,680,154
1798	7,786,670	292,909
1799	9,483,856	(1,749,005)
1800	11,027,995	34,778
1801	34,457,232	3,541,831
1802	8,258,168	7,019,542
1803	8,274,651	3,111,811
1804	8,975,410	3,188,400
1805	9,391,716	4,546,344

1806	9,866,412	6,110754
1807	8,808,036	8,043,868
1808	9,524,241	7,999,249
1809	10,778,759	(2,507,274)
1810	8,970,722	909,461
1811	8677140	(6,244,594)
1812	20,820,936	(10,479,639)
1813	32,362,864	(17,341,442)
1814	35,448,052	(23,539,300)
1815	33,691,782	(17,246,744)
1816	32,000,778	16,480,020
1817	20,907,407	13,108,158
1818	21,054,460	1,566,545
1819	22,629,865	3,091,370
1820	19,446,461	(4,444,805)
1821	17,032,476	(1,276,173)
1822	16,157,298	5,231,996
1823	15,876,515	5,834,036
1824	21,442,902	892,490
1825	17,063,802	5,983,641
1826	18,347,175	8,222,575

1827	17,512,407	6,827,197
1828	18,018,175	8,368,787
1829	16,966,186	9.643,574
1830	17,074,816	9,702,008
1831	17,173,940	13,289,004
1832	19,555,122	
1833	25,947,967	10,930,874
1834	21,538,175	17,857,274
1836	33,709,930	19,958,632
1837	40,531,533	(12,289,061)
1838	38,295,377	(7,562,153)
1839	31,533,319	4,585,067
1840	29,032,754	4,834,403
1841	30,889,544	(9,621,658)
1844	26,720,848	6,837,148
1845	27,225,670	7,034,278
1846	30,748,382	2,438,785
1847	58,801,093	(28,453,381)
1848	52,173,432	(11,989,521)
1849	48,204,255	(12,778,001)
1850	46,448,368	2,644,506

1851	54,162,083	4,803,561
1852	49,574,778	5,456,563
1853	52,984,714	13,843,043
1854	61,294,041	18,761,886
1855	65,272,799	6,719,912
1856	75,647,172	5,330,349
1857	74,988,361	1,330,904
1858	81,469,288	(27,827,127)
1859	76,962,084	(16,216,492)
1860	71,718,943	(7,146,276)
1861	74,999,509	(25,173,973)
1862	477,870,062	(417,650,980)
1863	729,898,066	(606,039,331)
1864	877,407,355	(621,556,130)
1865	1,309,655,448	(978,068,131)
1866	533,459,342	927,208
1867	362,026,353	116,117,354
1868	386,631,735	6,095,320
1869	339,535,108	35,997,659
1870	313,429,226	102,302,820
1871	303,197,439	91,270,711

1872	292,475,122	94,134,534
1873	308,236,007	36,938,349
1874	327,709,872	(1,297,710)
1875	301,414,754	9,397,379
1876	293,745,282	24,965,500
1877	268,866,060	39,666,167
1878	266,241,844	20,482,450
1879	296,989,866	5,374,253
1880	298,163,117	68,678,863
1881	296,437,037	101,130,654
1882	299,857,850	145,543,811
1883	310,916,830	132,879,444
1884	287,452,203	104,393,625
1885	302,787,779	63,463,771
1886	286,431,561	63,463,771
1887	316,769,780	93,956,588
1888	312,349,136	103,471,098
1889	338,172,227	119,612,116
1890	358,618,585	105,344,496
1891	421,304,471	37,239,763
1892	415,953,806	9,914,454

1893	459,374,947	2,341,674
1894	442,605,759	(69,803,261)
1895	433,178,426	42,805,223)
1896	434,678,654	(25,203,246)
1897	448,439,623	(18,052,454)
1898	532,381,202	(38,047,247)
1899	700,093,564	(89,111,560)
1900	590,068,371	79,527,060
1901	621,598546	77,717840
1902	593,038,905	91,287,375
1903	640,323,450	54,297,667
1904	725,984,946	(41,770,572)
1905	720,105,498	(23,004,228)
1906	736,717,582	25,669,323

The following is a separate U.S. Census Bureau report of Federal Expenditures Surpluses or (Deficits)

1908	(57,334,000)
1909	(89,423,000)
1910	((18,105,000)
1911	10,631,000
1912	2,728,000
1913	(401,000)

1914	(408,000)
1915	62,676,000
1916	48,478
1917	(853,357,000)
1918	(9,032,120,000)
1919	(13,362,623,000)
1920	291,222,000
1921	509,005,000
1922	736,496,000
1923	712,508,100
1924	963,367,000
1925	717,043,000
1926	865,144,000
1927	1,135,365,000
1928	939,083,000
1929	734,391,000
1930	737,673,000
1931	(461,877,000)
1932	(2,735,290,000)
1933	(2,601,652,000)
1934	(3,629,532,000)

1935	(2,791,052,000)
1936	(4,424,549,000)
1937	(2,777,421,000)
1938	(1,176,617,000)
1939	(3,362,158,000)

The following is a separate U.S. Census Bureau report of Federal Expenditure Surpluses or (Deficits)

1956	4,100,000,000
1957	3,200,000,000
1958	(2,900,000,000)
1959	(12,900,000,000)
1961	(3,400,000,000)
1962	(7,100,000,000)
1963	(4,800,000,000)
1964	(5,900,000,000)
1965	(1,600,000,000)
1966	(3,800,000,000)
1967	(8,700,000,000)
1968	(25,200,000,000)
1969	3,200,000,000
1970	(2,800,000,000)

Appendix C

Senate Vacancies due to Deadlocks in State Legislatures

Montana	1893
Washington	1893
Wyoming	1893
Delaware	1895
Oregon	1897
Delaware	1899
California	1899
Pennsylvania	1899
Utah	1899
Delaware 1	1899
Delaware	1905

Appendix D

Demands from States for Direct Election of Senators

Nebraska	1893
Minnesota	1901
Pennsylvania	1901
Idaho	1901
Montana	1901, 1905
Oregon	1901, 1903, 1909
Tennessee	1901,1905
Colorado	1901
Michigan	1901
Texas	1901
Arkansas	1901
Kentucky	1902
Illinois	1903, 1907
Nevada	1903
New Jersey	1907
Louisiana	1908

Oklahoma	1908
Kansas	1909
Wisconsin	1910
Montana	1911
Maine	1911
California	1911

Appendix E

Speeches in Congress on Direct Election of Senators

Speeches in favor of direct election:

David Turpie, Democrat, Indiana Dec 17 1891

John Palmer, Democrat, Illinois April 12 1892

David Turpie, Democrat, Indiana Feb. 6 1892

John H. Mitchell, Repub., June 5 1896

John M Palmer, Democrat Illinois June 5 1896

David Turpie, Democrat Indiana March 23, 1897

Joseph W Bailey Democrat May 8, 1902

William Jennings Bryan Nebraska July 12 1892, July 20, 1894 Democrat

Speeches against the direct election

George R Hoar, Massachusetts April 6 and 7 1893 Republican

W R Chandler, June 5 1896 Republican

George R Hoar, March 11 1902 Republican

C. M Depew, New York April 10 1902 Republican

George R Hoar, May 9 1902 Republican

George G Vest, Missouri June 11 1902 Democrat

Appendix F

Federal Income Tax Brackets

1913-2013

Brackets and Tax Rate Range Changes

Revenue Act 1913

1913   1%   7%

Income <$20,000   Income> $500,000

Revenue Act 1916 Bracket and Rate Change

Income< $4,000   Income> 1,000,000

1919   4%   73%

Revenue Act 1921 Bracket and Rate Change

1922   4%   58%

Income <$4,000 Income> $200,000

Revenue Act 1924 Bracket and Rate Change

Income< $4,000 Income> $500,000

1925   1.5%   25%

Bracket Change Income <$4,000 · Income> $100,000

1926   1.5%   25%

1928   1.5%   25%

Revenue Act 1932 Bracket and Rate Change

<$4,000   >$1,000,000

| 1932 | 4% | 63% |

Revenue Act 1936 Bracket and Rate Change

| 1936 | 4% | 79% |

<$4,000   >5,000,000

Revenue Act 1940 and Rate Change

| 1941 | 10% | 81% |

Revenue Act 1941 Bracket and Rate Change

$2,000   >$5,000,000

| 1942 | 19% | 88% |

Revenue Act 1942 Bracket Change

<$2,000   >$200,000

Revenue Act 1944 Rate Change

| 1944 | 23% | 94% |
| 1945 | 23% | 94% |

IRS Code 1945 Rate Change

| 1946 | 20% | 91% |

Revenue Act 1948 Bracket Change

<$4,000   >$400,000

Tax Reform Act 1964 Bracket and Rate Change

>$1,000   >$200,000

1964	16%	77%	
1965	14%	70%	

Tax Reform Act 1969 Bracket and Exemption Change

	>$1,000	$100,000	
1970	14%	70%	Incomes up to $1,000 exempt
1977	14%	70%	Incomes up to $2,100 exempt
1978	14%	70%	Incomes up to $2,100 exempt
	>$3,400	>$215,400	
1979	14%	70%	Incomes up to $2,300 exempt

Economic Recovery Tax Act 1981 Bracket and Rate Change

1981	14%	70%	Incomes up to $2,300 exempt
1982	12%	50% Incomes up to $2,300 exempt	

Tax Equity and Fiscal Responsibility Act 1982 Bracket and Rate Change

	>$3,400	>$85,600	
1983	11%	50% Incomes up to $2,300 exempt	
	>$3,400	>$162,400	

Tax Reform Act of 1984 Bracket Change

1985	11%	50%
>$3,670		>$175,250

Tax Reform Act of 1986 Bracket and Rate Change

1987	11%	38.5%

>$3,000   >$90,000

Omnibus Budget Reconciliation Act 1990 Bracket and Rate Change

1991   15%   31%

        $34,000   >$82,150

1992   15%   31%

Omnibus Budget Reconciliation Act of 1993 Bracket and Rate Change

1993   15%   39.6%

$38,000   >$250,000

1995   15%   39.6%

        $39,000 >$256,500

2000   15%   39.6%

        $43,850   >$288,350

Economic Growth and Tax Relief Reconciliation Act of 2001 Bracket and Rate Change

2001   15%   39.1%

2002   10%   38.6%

12,000   >$307,050

Jobs Growth Tax Relief Reconciliation Act of 2003 Bracket and Rate Change

2003   10%   35%

$7,150   >$319,100

American Taxpayer Relief Act of 2012 Bracket and Rate Change

2012	10%	35%
2013	10%	39.6%
$8,925		>$400,001

Appendix G

Historical Data on Federal Debt as % of GDP

Year	Debt % GDP
1790	29.6
1795	18.7
1800	15.1
1805	10.9
1810	6.2
1815	10.2
1820	8.3
1825	6.5
1830	3.2
1835	0
1840	.3
1845	.7
1850	2.3
1855	.9
1860	1.9
1865	31.0

1870	27.9
1875	23.7
1880	18.4
1885	13.2
1890	7.8
1895	7.9
1900	6.6
1905	4.3
1910	3.7
1915	3.3
1920	27.3
1925	21.6
1930	16.5
1935	42.9
1940	42.7
1945	112.7
1950	73.7
1955	55.5
1960	44.8
1965	36.5
1969	28.5

1975	26.6
1980	26.2
1985	37.1
1990	42.8
1995	49.2
2000	34.5

Source; Congressional Budget Office

Appendix H

Government Receipts as % of GDP

Federal v State and Local

Year	Federal %	State &Local
1930	3.4	9.1*
1940	9.6	9.4*
1950	14.1	6.1
1960	17.3	7.1
1970	18.4	8.9
1980	18.5	8.6
1990	17.4	9.3
2000	20.0	9.6
2010	14.6	9.6
2014	17.5	9.5

Sources: 1930-2014 Table 1.2 and 14.3 white house.gov/omb/budget/historicals

*source of State and local for 1930 and 1940 from tax foundation.org

Display a brushed antique gold plastic, engraved, magnetic bumper sticker for your car. The author purchased this bumper sticker displayed in full color on the cover art from an American Wisconsin craftsman at info@customengravingshop.com.

Harley's Custom Clocks and Laser Engraving
www.customengravingshop.com.

The artist can create custom signs for any cause or event,

Also by Cheryl Poule:

<u>Vengeance of Tyrants</u>

A historical tale of the real progressive and socialist attack on American culture and religion. The 130 year American experience includes the true history of the manipulation of American education, law, medicine and religion by social scientists. The oppression of Russian civilians and the celebration by progressive Americans of the communist revolution is told from the perspective of ordinary citizens. The social impact in America of the progressive changes in our culture is described from the perspective of Americans who witnessed the changes.

The following is an excerpt

from Chapter One of <u>Vengeance of Tyrants</u>

The Jacksonian Era

1832-1850

1832, Boston, Goddet Cottage

The "Blue Death;" Beatrice thought as she looked at her mother, Marie Goddet's face. It was the term for cholera due to the effect on the patient. *How much more fluid can she lose?* Beatrice thought after tossing the third bucket.

The cholera epidemic had begun in India 25 years earlier. It had moved halfway around the world, as it contaminated rivers and water wells. The epidemic would finally die in the American wilderness after killing thousands in the Midwest.

Beatrice passed the bed where her father's blue body laid waiting for burial. *Where is Daniel*, she wondered. Her brother had left hours ago to look for a burial plot. He had eagerly volunteered in order to get out of the morbid home. Beatrice, only sixteen years old, was alone with her father's corpse and her dying mother.

Decades later scientists would recognize cholera as a clever and vicious killer. The bacteria shields itself in the victim's stomach, grows "spears" of chemicals that penetrate the intestinal wall. The collapse of the intestinal wall from the chemical injury results in massive diarrhea. Diarrhea was the leading cause of death in the century.

Beatrice wasn't concerned for herself, she was unusually immune to illness. Medical books of the century referred to women as "natural invalids." The average woman had seven babies, of which only three would survive. One out of ten Americans would die of tuberculosis by age 50. Scarlet fever, diphtheria, measles and mumps would also attack and maim children.

A weak voice startled Beatrice. "Please keep this with you to defend against the tyrants." Her mother offered her the cherished Richard Baxter book, <u>A Christian Directory</u>. [148] This book, one of five volumes of Baxter's writings, had been treasured by her family as a source of wisdom.

Beatrice's parents had come to America after Maximillien's 1793 *Reign of Terror* in France when Christianity was criminalized, priests were executed and churches converted into *Temples of Reason*. The nationalist wars against religion began in France, but the ideas were germinated in Germany.

Mrs. Goddet knew the likely source of her infection. *It was the visitor from Germany at her landlord's house.* It was only a week ago when Martha, the landlord's daughter banged on the door. "Mrs. Goddet, come look at the visiting professor, Dr. Rudolf Esser. He is quite ill." Mrs. Goddet was known for her knowledge of herbal medicines. The landlord, Mr. Fontaine, preferred to remain quiet about the diarrhea illness in his home. His wife was hosting a reception next week.

---

[148] Baxter, Richard, <u>A Christian Directory, or a Body of Practical Divinity and Cases of Conscience</u>, Vol. 5, London; Richard Evans, 1825,(Richard Baxter, a Puritan theologian of the 1600's wrote it 200 years earlier.)

Boston, Fontaine Estate, a week earlier

Mrs. Goddet had observed the pale and thin man in her landlord's home, and noted an odor of diarrhea and vomiting. She felt his head, "You have a fever. Are you chilled?" she asked Professor Esser. She was careful not to sit between the patient and the fire in case the disease was attracted to the heat. Using the same caution of the times, she had eaten before arriving.

"Oui," he answered in response to her French accent. She noted his German accent in his attempt to speak French. "When did you come to America?" he asked.

"About thirty years ago I escaped France" she said.

"Escaped? You should have stayed. France is a much more lawful and civil nation now." He said boldly.

"It wasn't safe for us" she said guardedly. "Worship was outlawed even in private. My friends who protected priests and nuns were executed."

"You were protecting religious leaders?" he asked "Why couldn't you accept the new civic religion, *Cult of the Supreme Being*?

"My faith is of the Bible" she replied, with restraint.

"You people must allow the superior scientific talents to lead."

"I have administered an antidote. Do you want me to pray for you?" Mrs. Goddet asked, ignoring his comment.

Dr. Esser had enough. He pushed his hand on her apron and said, "Get away from me with your superstition. Isn't there a scientist in this town?" Esser asked Mr. Fontaine brazenly.

Boston, Goddet Cottage

A few days later Mrs. Goddet's husband became ill. She said "Here is an antidote I gave to the professor, a mixture of cayenne pepper, tincture of opium, rhubarb, peppermint and camphor." Unlike the professor, her faithful and devoted husband did not recover.

Boston, Fontaine Estate, a week later

At the landlord's home the German professor, Dr. Rudolf Esser, was recovering from his illness. "I missed my transportation to New Harmony. I was hoping to teach with my colleagues in the Indiana community. I left my faculty position in Germany for this." He complained to Mr. Fontaine.

"I read about the *Boatload of Knowledge*. A boat full of the best scientists headed to the New Harmony utopian community." Mr. Fontaine said.

"Yes, Robert Owen, from Scotland, conceived a social utopia based on science, not religion, and where there is social and gender equality." Esser said boasting.

"Perhaps you should consider establishing a school in Boston." Mr. Fontaine advised Prof. Esser. "I can arrange for your introduction to the leading members of our community."

"Your country does need citizens better prepared to do service for the State. They need to be taught cohesiveness and social order for the benefit of all. There is too much free will here." The professor told him conceitedly.

Boston, Goddet Cottage

Mrs. Goddet lay dying. She whispered urgently to Beatrice, "I regret not telling you about the dark forces of tyranny. Remember the *Reign of Terror*. Will you recognize tyranny? Stay close to Daniel. He will protect your independence, you will protect his spirit. Are you listening?"

Beatrice was inattentive. Marie Goddet rested her head in disappointment and thought about the tyranny of powerful men against ordinary families.

Mrs. Goddet remembered how the tyrants had gained power over France and destroyed church property. Before the tyrants finished they had destroyed freedom for the faithful population. No one knew where the tyrants derived their power.

Marie Goddet felt the light of life dimming and hurriedly picked up the ink well and quill and wrote in her Bible, "Terror, vengeance, tyrants…" She dropped her quill.

Suddenly she was in peace, free from doubts and fears.

Beatrice was still distracted. "It will be okay. We are in America now." Beatrice said, smoothing her mother'shead. She felt a hot tingle in her arm that moved toward her heart.

Beatrice was startled by a noise near the door. *Hopefully it is someone to take the burden from me. I am emotionally numbed already. I cannot tolerate another loss alone.*

 "Daniel, is that you?" She listened desperately for her brother, but there was no answer. Beatrice assumed they would need two burial plots soon. She looked out the window and saw the boy Thomas in the barn with Cody, their pony. Every night the odd, mal-formed, lonely boy visited their pony and sometimes slept in the stall. She could see him in the full moonlight. "Thomas is an odd boy. What is it about him and that pony?" Beatrice spoke quietly to her mother, not realizing she could no longer hear.

Boston, Fontaine Estate

Daniel Goddet, Beatrice's brother, was almost home. He started walking backward away from the babbling Martha, the landlord's daughter. "My sister is waiting for me." He pleaded as he walked downhill toward the cottage.

Martha wanted him to linger. She hoped her friends would see her talking with him. All the girls admired Daniel. He had brown hair like silk parted in the middle. His clothes fit perfectly on his muscular body. Martha would watch in her room for Daniel to approach and waited by the gate for a chance conversation. Daniel always daydreamed about his future as a hunter and pioneer and didn't notice Martha's frequent interference.

Boston, Goddet Cottage

Beatrice looked up the hill toward the Fontaine's home. She could see Martha holding a candle and talking to someone. Beatrice hoped that when Daniel returned, Martha would visit her. *I could use a friend now, but is she really a friend?* Beatrice had not inherited Daniel's silky hair, fine skin or straight teeth. There was no admirer to watch Beatrice stroll down the lane.

Beatrice turned toward her mother's bed and opened the Rev. Baxter book to read again. Beatrice looked at her mother and finally realized she was not breathing. "No" she screamed as she bent over the chair. She felt her soul shatter. Daniel and Thomas heard the shriek from outside the house and froze, neither was anxious to assist.

Finally, Beatrice heard the door open and slam. "Daniel? They are both gone. Did you get a grave plot?" Beatrice asked desperately.

"Yeah," he paused, "but we better do it tonight" Daniel replied. *I couldn't find anyone who would talk to me about purchasing a plot. I will have to dig in the pauper's section,* he thought.

"Should we get the pastor?" Beatrice asked urgently.

"No time, he is out on the circuit" Daniel replied. *Actually, I am not sure about the circuit, but I know I don't want to waste time,* he thought. *I have to keep busy so I don't think about this awful day.*

"Maybe Thomas will help us?" Beatrice asked Daniel.

"Watermelon head? I doubt it." Daniel replied with contempt.

"Please, don't call him that." Beatrice said. She always felt sympathy for anyone or anything who was mistreated. She felt like a guardian for the weak.

Daniel shrugged at Beatrice's appeal. *This is why I have to leave here*, he thought. It wasn't his fault he did not have the ability to empathize. His family always expected him to feel emotion.

From the stable, the lonely boy, Thomas had watched the activity in the house. The pony seemed disturbed by the events. He soothed the pony "It will be alright. We will stay together." Thomas could not tolerate losing Cody. "I will never let you be hurt again" he told the pony and looked at the hoof.

Thomas was the oldest boy in his family and the biggest disappointment to his pa. He was physically large, especially his head. He was not gifted with coordination or added intelligence in spite of his large head. He was clumsy and often broke small parts with his oversized muscles. Three years ago he decided to practice shoeing a pony. He didn't tell anyone. No one would have permitted it. It was a very sad harrier performance. "I should have used smaller nails and shorter shoes. I am sorry I hurt you so bad." He looked at the scarred hoof. "I shouldn't have tried to fix it either." He never told anyone what he had done.

Everyone wondered who tried to shoe the pony? The pony had a bad limp for months.

"You never blamed me did you? You are my one and only friend." Whenever Thomas had a typical bad day he found solace with Cody in the stable. Beatrice's parents didn't seem to mind. Thomas's large family didn't seem to miss him. He felt at home in the stable.

Thomas watched Beatrice and Daniel walk to the cemetery. Thomas hugged the pony. As Daniel had thought, Thomas didn't leave the stable or offer to help.

No one was on the street. During an epidemic, everyone kept to themselves in their own homes. At the time, residents believed diseases were caused by bad air. The rumors about the recent blue deaths had begun to circulate.

Daniel looked around the cemetery, "This will do" and he dug a hole big enough for two bodies between two small wooden crosses. Beatrice wound a vine around two sticks in the shape of a cross.

They dropped the board holding their deceased parents above the hole. It shifted to the right. Her father was leaning on her mother. *It was appropriate*, Beatrice thought. Beatrice tried to read from the Bible but it was too dark even in the moonlight. Daniel shuffled impatiently waiting to fill the hole.

Beatrice cried while she buried her hopes and her family. They walked home in silence.

They were orphans with no family on this side of the Atlantic Ocean. They only had each other. *Who would care about their future, their life story?* Beatrice wondered. They had grown up together, only a year apart in age but miles apart in character. They both wondered about the future. Daniel dreamed of freedom and independence. Beatrice dreamed of family and commitment.

Boston, Fontaine Estate

The leading members of the community were invited to dinner to meet with the visiting German professor about starting a college.   While they were socializing, Mr. Fontaine and Dr. Esser observed the odd activities at the rental cottage. "Come take a look." Mr. Fontaine showed Dr. Esser his telescope he used to monitor his tenants. They did not mention the morbid events to the others for fear of damping the enjoyment of the evening.

Professor Esser had no difficulty re-focusing his attention on his personal mission. "In German schools we are teaching social obedience and moral world order of Johann Gottlieb Fichte[149]. These philosophies of social obedience will be useful for our citizens in every academic discipline." Professor Esser told the guests at dinner.

"I have never heard of him," a guest said skeptically.

"That is because you weren't educated in Germany. We lead the world through our reformation in general national education and teacher training." Professor Esser said pompously and belched.

---

[149] Johann Gottlieb Fichte (1762-1814) Chair, Univ. Berlin 1810. Considered a "Father of Modern German Nationalism". In an Address to the German Nation, he wrote, "The German art of the State understands that it cannot create this spirit by reprimanding adults who are already spoilt by neglect but only by educating the young, who are unspoilt."